# COGAT
## GRADE 5
### LEVEL 11

# Test Preparation

**BoldBells**

# Table of Content

# Introduction

CogAT test is designed to measure student's academic aptitude and cognitive development. This test is frequently used to identify and admit children into a school's gifted and talented program.

CogAT test assess a child's reasoning or cognitive ability in three key section or areas. verbal battery, nonverbal battery, and quantitative battery

**Verbal Battery:** This battery assesses a student's verbal thinking abilities, which include their ability to comprehend, remeber, use and modify English words, phrases, and sentences.

**Quantitative :** This battery assesses a student's quantitative reasoning abilities, including their understanding of basic numerical concepts, relationships between numbers and solving equations.

**Non-Verbal battery:** This battery assesses a student's figural reasoning abilities. It focuses on a student's ability to recognize patterns, shapes, icons, sequences, and relationships without using language.

# The Sections of the CogAT Test and CogAT Questions Examples

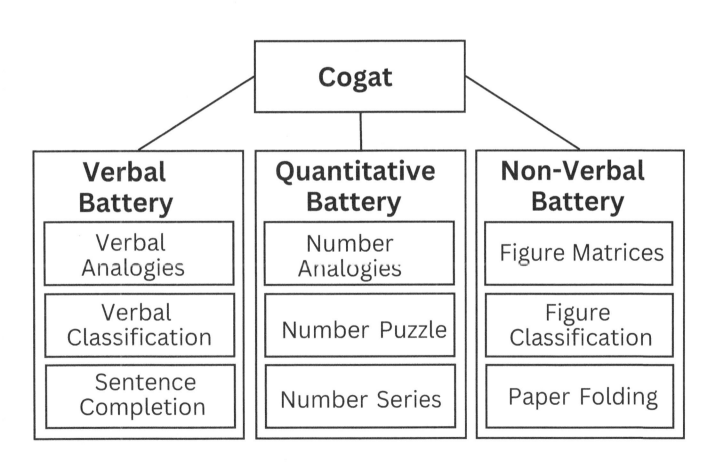

# Verbal Battery

## Verbal Analogy

A verbal analogy question begins with word pairs. These pairs consist of words that have a certain relationship with each other. The first and second words in the pair have a relationship with each other, as do the third and fourth word. The students will be given 1st, 2nd and 3rd words then asked to choose the word that goes with the third word the same way that the second word goes with the first.

{First word} - {second Word} : {third word} - {Fourth Word}

## Example

1. Fish → Gills :Human → _____
    a. Neck
    b. Head
    c. Intestine
    d. Lungs
    e. Liver

In this example, Lungs is the right answer. Fish uses gills to breath underwater, human use lungs to breath

# Answering Verbal analogies questions

Understanding the relationships between the first two words will help students approach verbal analogies questions with confidence.

Common relationship are;

- Synonyms and Antonyms
- Function
- Use or Purpose
- Cause and Effect
- Attribute
- Opposite Action

# Sentence Completion

Sentence Completion This subtest category of the verbal battery helps to measures student's understanding of English vocabulary and how to use it correctly. The child needs to read or listen to the questions and choose the missing word or words from the given options.

## Example

Andy swore an _ _ _ _ _ _ and assure to tell the truth

(A) word  (B) statement  (C) oath  (D) cast  (E) truth

In this example, Oath is the right answer.

## Verbal Classification

Verbal Classification is about figuring out how words are alike and sorting them based on those similarities.

The students will be given a list of three words that have something in common. They will be asked to choose a word from the given options that also has similar thing in common with the three words.

## Example

Tired,  Worn out,  Exhausted

(A) enormous  (B) distrust  (C) solace  (D) fatigued (E) spider

In this example, Fatigued is the right answer. All the words meaning are the same.

# Verbal Battery

## Number analogies

This subtest category of the Quantitative battery assess students numerical reasoning skills and problem-solving abilities.

The student will be given 3 set of numbers, two completed sets and the third set with a missing number. they will be ask to find the relationship between the first two sets of numbers and then choose a number from the answer choices which follows the same pattern when paired with the number in the third set.

## Example

1. [42 – 6]   [63 – 9]    [105 – __ ]

   (A) 15  (B) 28  (C) 35  (D) 42  (E) 115

In this example, the first number is divided by 7, so the correct answer is (A) 15.

2. [43 – 60]   [32 – 49]    [54 – __ ]

   (A) 62  (B) 71  (C) 48  (D) 57  (E) 79

In this example, 17 is added to the first number, so the correct answer is (B) 71.

# Number series

Number series subtest category assess students logical thinking ability.

The student is given a series of numbers and they are asked to figure out which number comes next in the series.

## Example

1. 2  6  18  54  162
   (A) 250  (B) 486  (C) 357  (D) 386  (E) 324

In this example, each number is multiplied by 3 to obtain the next number. The correct answer is (B) 486.

2. 73  65  57  49  41
   (A) 29  (B) 33  (C) 25  (D) 46  (E) 39

In this example, 8 is subtracted from each numbers to get the next number. The right answer is (B) 33

# Number Puzzles

Number Puzzles questions are like math riddles, but with a twist: they're a bit like algebra questions where you need to find the value of an unknown number.

The student is given an equation with symbols. They are asked to use the information provided to solve the equation and choose a number from the given options that will replace the symbol.

## Example

1.   30 = ? + 12

   (A) 18  (B) 22  (C) 40  (D) 17  (E) 15

In this example, the first thing to notice is that the numbers on the either side of the equation must be equal.

To solve this, we are to subtract 12 from the both sides of the equation

30 - 12 = ? + 12 - 12

30 - 12 = ?

? = 18

The correct answer is (A) 18

2.   2 + 6 = ? x 4

   (A) 5  (B) 7  (C) 2  (D) 15  (E) 10

In this example, the first thing to notice is that the numbers on the either side of the equation must be equal.

To solve this, we are to divide both side by 4

$$2 + 6 = ? \times 4$$

$$2 + 6 \div 4 = ? \times 4 \div 4$$

$$(2+6) \div 4$$

$$8 \div 4 = 2$$

The correct answer is (C) 2

# Non-Verbal battery

## Figure Matrices

This subtest category of the Non-Verbal battery access a student's non-verbal reasoning abilities. The understanding of shapes and symbols that are related through a rule.

Students will be given series of visual figures arranged in a matrix. These figures can be vary in term of shapes, line, colors and arrangements. Within the matrix, one of the figures is missing.

The students' are asked to find out the hidden rule or connection between the figures in the matrix and select the correct answer from the given options that correctly completes the matrix.

# Example

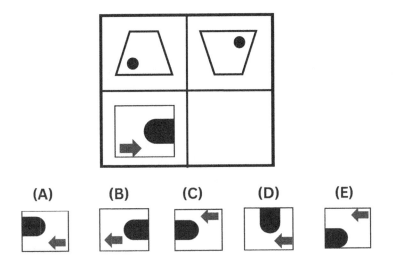

In this example, the correct answer is (C) the figures rotate 180 degree clockwise.

# Figure classification

Students are shown a series of figures, which are arranged in rows or groups. These figures can vary in terms of shapes, lines, colors, and arrangements.

The students are asked to identify the common relationship or connection that binds the figures within each row or group and pick the figure that fits with them from the given options.

# Example

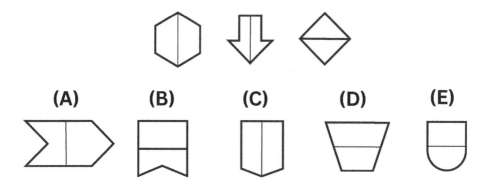

In this example, the correct answer is (C) the figures are divided into two equal parts.

# Paper folding

This assessment measures non-verbal reasoning and spatial intelligence.

Students are to figure out how a hole-punched paper will appear when unfolded. they are to select the right answers from the given options.

# Example

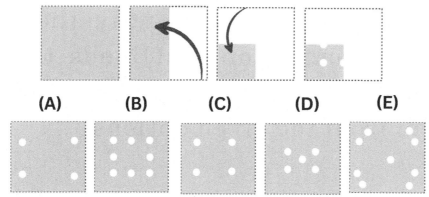

In this example, the correct answer is (b)

11

# How to use this book

This book is designed to help parents/teachers familiarize their child/students with the test format, improve their cognitive abilities, and boost their confidence.

- This book has 2 full length Cogat Level 9 practice questions.
- Start the practice together with your child with the Practice 1.
- Read the direction on every subtest category practice for your child so they can understand what each section is all about.
- Check the back pages for the answers key and answer sheet .
- Ensure to read the explanations for any questions they got wrong and explain what makes it the right answer.
- Allow your child to go through practice 2 on their own. This is to know how well they've improved after the guidance you provided in the test 1.

# Practice 1

# Verbal Analogies

In the verbal analogies subtest, there is a relationship between the first pair of words. You are to identify this relationship and then choose the pair of words that has a similar relationship.

1. Lion ⟶ Lioness : Horse ⟶ _____

   Ⓐ mare  Ⓑ falcon  Ⓒ hen  Ⓓ doe  Ⓔ *goose*

2. Centimeter ⟶ Cm : Gram ⟶ _____

   Ⓐ kg  Ⓑ m  Ⓒ g  Ⓓ gb  Ⓔ m

3. Banana ⟶ peel : Nut ⟶ _____

   Ⓐ pud  Ⓑ coat  Ⓒ cover  Ⓓ back  Ⓔ shell

4. Thermometer ⟶ Temperature : Barometer ⟶ _____

   Ⓐ photometer  Ⓑ Air pressure  Ⓒ liquid  Ⓓ solid

   Ⓔ forecast

5. Chicken ⟶ Hen : Cat ⟶ _____

Ⓐ tom    Ⓑ doe    Ⓒ queen    Ⓓ jenny    Ⓔ bull

6. Wonderful ⟶ Good : Terrifying ⟶ _____

Ⓐ Amazing    Ⓑ sad    Ⓒ awesome    Ⓓ frightening
Ⓔ experience

7. Cub ⟶ Bear : Bunny ⟶ _____

Ⓐ giraffe    Ⓑ tiger    Ⓒ rabbit    Ⓓ swan    Ⓔ sheep

8. Six ⟶ Hexagon : Eight ⟶ _____

Ⓐ pentagon    Ⓑ octagon    Ⓒ triangle    Ⓓ decagon    Ⓔ circle

9. Easy ⟶ Simple : Difficult ⟶ _____

Ⓐ relaxed    Ⓑ secure    Ⓒ safe    Ⓓ complex    Ⓔ serene

10. France ⟶ Country : Polish ⟶ _____

Ⓐ city    Ⓑ language    Ⓒ food    Ⓓ culture    Ⓔ state

11. Preserve ⟶ Maintain : Brave ⟶ _____

Ⓐ loyal  Ⓑ courageous  Ⓒ mad  Ⓓ serious  Ⓔ beast

12. Teacher ⟶ Teach : Scientist ⟶ _____

Ⓐ view  Ⓑ operate  Ⓒ research  Ⓓ admister  Ⓔ sign

13. Lizard ⟶ Reptile : dolphin ⟶ _____

Ⓐ fish  Ⓑ mammals  Ⓒ insect  Ⓓ bird  Ⓔ animal

14. Artist ⟶ brush : barber ⟶ _____

Ⓐ screw  Ⓑ pipe  Ⓒ pliers  Ⓓ car jack  Ⓔ scissors

15. Maternal ⟶ Mother : Paternal ⟶ _____

Ⓐ friend  Ⓑ father  Ⓒ uncle  Ⓓ sister  Ⓔ patient

16. Amaze ⟶ Surprise : love ⟶ _____

Ⓐ loyal  Ⓑ funny  Ⓒ belief  Ⓓ amusing  Ⓔ affection

17. Victory ⟶ Defeat :   Pain ⟶ _____

Ⓐ Calm   Ⓑ relief   Ⓒ loyal   Ⓓ local   Ⓔ foe

18. Microphone ⟶ Singer : Racket ⟶ _____

Ⓐ sprinter   Ⓑ cyclists   Ⓒ tennis player   Ⓓ gymnasts
Ⓔ boxers

19. Tired ⟶ Exhausted : Happy ⟶ _____

Ⓐ Serious   Ⓑ guilty   Ⓒ defeat   Ⓓ unhappy   Ⓔ cheerful

20. Friend ⟶ Foe : Brave ⟶ _____

Ⓐ coward   Ⓑ enemy   Ⓒ courage   Ⓓ laugh   Ⓔ easy

# Verbal Classification

In the verbal classification subtest, you will be provided with group of words. You are to identify the word in the given options that belongs to the group of words based on a specific relationship. It could be a category, a characteristic, or any other logical connection between words.

1. Mercury, Jupiter, Saturn, _____
   Ⓐ Planet
   Ⓑ Sky
   Ⓒ Space
   Ⓓ Neptune
   Ⓔ Wave

2. Success, Victory, Win, _____
   Ⓐ Defeat
   Ⓑ Confident
   Ⓒ Guilty
   Ⓓ Happy
   Ⓔ Triumph

3. Yam, onion, potato, _____
   Ⓐ Mango
   Ⓑ Apple
   Ⓒ Carrots
   Ⓓ Banana
   Ⓔ Maize

4. Chameleon,  Snake, Lizard,  _____

    Ⓐ Dolphin
    Ⓑ Spider
    Ⓒ leopard
    Ⓓ Bear
    Ⓔ Turtle


5. Brave,  Courageous, Fearless,  _____

    Ⓐ irritable
    Ⓑ Valiant
    Ⓒ tedious
    Ⓓ dull
    Ⓔ tough


6. Dog,  Toad,  Leopard,  _____

    Ⓐ Chicken
    Ⓑ Koala
    Ⓒ Dolphin
    Ⓓ Snake
    Ⓔ Eels


7. Spain, Canada, Mexico,  _____

    Ⓐ Language
    Ⓑ Country
    Ⓒ Germany
    Ⓓ French
    Ⓔ culture


8. Single,  lone,  Solitary,  _____

    Ⓐ Solo
    Ⓑ Double
    Ⓒ Family
    Ⓓ Group
    Ⓔ Together

9. Wheat, Sorghum, Oats, _____
   Ⓐ Bread
   Ⓑ Bakery
   Ⓒ Cake
   Ⓓ Rice
   Ⓔ Porridge


10. Passion, Gratitude, Confidence, _____
    Ⓐ Rude
    Ⓑ Happiness
    Ⓒ Fear
    Ⓓ Guilty
    Ⓔ Hurt


11. Sitar, Guitar, Violin, _____
    Ⓐ Flute
    Ⓑ Piano
    Ⓒ Drum
    Ⓓ Banjo
    Ⓔ Trombone


12. January, October, December, _____
    Ⓐ Febuary
    Ⓑ August
    Ⓒ Month
    Ⓓ Year
    Ⓔ Calendar


13. Happy, Cheerful, Joyful, _____
    Ⓐ Unhappy
    Ⓑ Delighted
    Ⓒ Dislike
    Ⓓ Stricken
    Ⓔ Composed

20

14. Thermometer, Stretcher, Stethoscope, _____
   A Syringes
   B Beaker
   C Jury Box
   D Biometrics
   E Clerk

15. Tiger, Dog, Wolf _____
   A Dove
   B Flamingos
   C Fish
   D Lizard
   E Bat

16. Frugal, thrifty, Careful, _____
   A Composed
   B Distrust
   C Pleased
   D Blameless
   E Prudent

17. Square, Rectangle, Triangle, _____
   A Shape
   B Circle
   C Figure
   D Drawing
   E Sign

18. Educator, Instructor, Professor, _____
   A Lawyer
   B Tutor
   C Nursing
   D Architect
   E Sponsor

19. Difficult, Strenuous, Hard, _____
   - (A) Tough
   - (B) Serious
   - (C) Comfort
   - (D) Tired
   - (E) Clear


20. Engine, Tail, Wing, _____
   - (A) Bow
   - (B) Sailor
   - (C) Cockpit
   - (D) Track
   - (E) Police

# Sentence Completion

In the sentence completion subtest, you are to select the right word to complete each sentence

1. My uncle's cow gave birth to three young _____
   Ⓐ Calf  Ⓑ Calfs  Ⓒ Calves  Ⓓ Cow  Ⓔ Lambs

2. The table was decorated with a _____ of flower
   Ⓐ Cup  Ⓑ Bouquet  Ⓒ Jar  Ⓓ Group  Ⓔ Many

3. The woman _____ came here is my maternal aunt
   Ⓐ Which  Ⓑ Where  Ⓒ whom  Ⓓ who  Ⓔ They

4. Isabella's father had \_\_\_\_\_ of the children when her parent divorced.
   Ⓐ Knowledge  Ⓑ Allocation  Ⓒ Custody  Ⓓ Attention
   Ⓔ Ownership

5. The house you are looking for is just \_\_\_\_\_ the corner
   Ⓐ Behind  Ⓑ Ahead  Ⓒ Alone  Ⓓ Around  Ⓔ above

6. Despite the storm, he decided to \_\_\_\_\_ the boat to rescue the stranded passenger.
   Ⓐ Drive  Ⓑ Sink  Ⓒ Ride  Ⓓ Hide  Ⓔ Sail

23

7. The scientist had to _____ various experiments to prove her ground breaking theory.
   Ⓐ Conduct  Ⓑ Apply  Ⓒ Invest  Ⓓ Ignore  Ⓔ Simplify

8. Despite the _____ she managed to solve the difficult math problem.
   Ⓐ Surge  Ⓑ Challenges  Ⓒ Hill  Ⓓ Abandon  Ⓔ Weight

9. To improve his vocabulary, he decided to _____ a new word everyday.
   Ⓐ Acquire  Ⓑ Written  Ⓒ Learn  Ⓓ Invest  Ⓔ Adjust

10. The church is just _____ the road
    Ⓐ behind  Ⓑ across  Ⓒ between  Ⓓ over  Ⓔ above

11. The chef had to follow the _____ carefully to create the perfect dish for the culinary.
    Ⓐ Flavor  Ⓑ Menu  Ⓒ Recipe  Ⓓ Guide  Ⓔ List

12. The Development of personal computers rendered Typewriters _____
    Ⓐ Preserve  Ⓑ Obsolete  Ⓒ useful  Ⓓ dismiss  Ⓔ Showcase

13. Andy swore an _____ and assure to tell the truth
    Ⓐ Word  Ⓑ Statement  Ⓒ Oath  Ⓓ Cast  Ⓔ True

14. The employer said the ability to operate a computer is _____ for the role.
    Ⓐ Crucial   Ⓑ overlook   Ⓒ express   Ⓓ Boast   Ⓔ Observe

15. We can _____ the prices of these two toys to see which one fits our budget.
    Ⓐ Amount   Ⓑ Different   Ⓒ Divide   Ⓓ Afford   Ⓔ Compare

16. Jerry Couldn't play soccer for a few weeks because he had a _____ in his arm.
    Ⓐ Cast   Ⓑ Wrinkle   Ⓒ Scratch   Ⓓ Fracture   Ⓔ Knock

17. The detective needed to _____ the finger prints found at the crime scene to identify the suspect.
    Ⓐ Explore   Ⓑ Analyze   Ⓒ Calculate   Ⓓ Solve
    Ⓔ Memorize

18. It's important to _____ your mistakes and learn from them to grow.
    Ⓐ Conduct   Ⓑ Modify   Ⓒ Remember   Ⓓ Accomplish
    Ⓔ Acknowledge

19. My sister is excited to go to _____ next year to study computer engineering.
    Ⓐ Office   Ⓑ City   Ⓒ University   Ⓓ society   Ⓔ abroad

20. We watched birds _____ through the garden in search of seeds and worm.

Ⓐ Tremble  Ⓑ Magnify  Ⓒ rummage  Ⓓ decay  Ⓔ Stable

# Number Analogy

In the number analogy subtest, there is a relationship between the pair of numbers. You are to identify the relationship and choose the right answer from the given options to complete the third pair of numbers

1. $[4 \rightarrow 08]$   $[7 \rightarrow 14]$   $[9 \rightarrow ?]$

Ⓐ 20   Ⓑ 35   Ⓒ 17   Ⓓ 15   Ⓔ 18

2. $[3 \rightarrow 12]$   $[5 \rightarrow 20]$   $[15 \rightarrow ?]$

Ⓐ 55   Ⓑ 60   Ⓒ 42   Ⓓ 33   Ⓔ 48

3. $[15 \rightarrow 22]$   $[48 \rightarrow 55]$   $[82 \rightarrow ?]$

Ⓐ 87   Ⓑ 49   Ⓒ 95   Ⓓ 89   Ⓔ 79

4. $[73 \rightarrow 86]$  $[81 \rightarrow 94]$  $[92 \rightarrow ?]$

(A) 120  (B) 105  (C) 110  (D) 142  (E) 98

5. $[42 \rightarrow 6]$  $[63 \rightarrow 9]$  $[105 \rightarrow ?]$

(A) 15  (B) 28  (C) 35  (D) 42  (E) 115

6. $[57 \rightarrow 34]$  $[49 \rightarrow 26]$  $[78 \rightarrow ?]$

(A) 62  (B) 55  (C) 82  (D) 79  (E) 68

7. $[29 \rightarrow 116]$  $[16 \rightarrow 64]$  $[31 \rightarrow ?]$

(A) 48  (B) 73  (C) 59  (D) 112  (E) 124

8. $[65 \rightarrow 13]$  $[40 \rightarrow 8]$  $[90 \rightarrow ?]$

(A) 25  (B) 18  (C) 39  (D) 28  (E) 42

9. $[43 \rightarrow 60]$  $[32 \rightarrow 49]$  $[54 \rightarrow ?]$

(A) 62  (B) 71  (C) 48  (D) 57  (E) 79

10. $[45 \rightarrow 15]$  $[60 \rightarrow 20]$  $[48 \rightarrow ?]$

(A) 19  (B) 32  (C) 28  (D) 16  (E) 18

11. $[88 \rightarrow 38]$    $[71 \rightarrow 21]$    $[69 \rightarrow ?]$

(A) 29    (B) 39    (C) 70    (D) 12    (E) 19

12. $[39 \rightarrow 45]$    $[88 \rightarrow 94]$    $[47 \rightarrow ?]$

(A) 49    (B) 57    (C) 53    (D) 35    (E) 41

13. $[49 \rightarrow 32]$    $[85 \rightarrow 68]$    $[67 \rightarrow ?]$

(A) 84    (B) 17    (C) 42    (D) 39    (E) 50

14. $[14 \rightarrow 70]$    $[20 \rightarrow 100]$    $[32 \rightarrow ?]$

(A) 120    (B) 112    (C) 160    (D) 150    (E) 156

15. $[45 \rightarrow 15]$    $[15 \rightarrow 5]$    $[75 \rightarrow ?]$

(A) 45    (B) 15    (C) 65    (D) 45    (E) 25

16. $[23 \rightarrow 17]$    $[42 \rightarrow 17]$    $[35 \rightarrow ?]$

(A) 17    (B) 28    (C) 35    (D) 11    (E) 19

17. $[49 \rightarrow 38]$    $[53 \rightarrow 42]$    $[38 \rightarrow ?]$

(A) 47    (B) 27    (C) 32    (D) 30    (E) 18

**18.** [17 → 34]    [24 → 48]    [34 → ?]

   Ⓐ 57    Ⓑ 39    Ⓒ 68    Ⓓ 42    Ⓔ 53

**19.** [64 → 39]    [73 → 48]    [81 → ?]

   Ⓐ 56    Ⓑ 42    Ⓒ 63    Ⓓ 59    Ⓔ 47

**20.** [19 → 34]    [43 → 58]    [38 → ?]

   Ⓐ 47    Ⓑ 30    Ⓒ 53    Ⓓ 67    Ⓔ 28

# Number Series

In the number series subtest, you are given a series of numbers that follows a certain pattern or rule. You are to find the missing number in the series

**1.** 16  23  30  37  44 ___

   Ⓐ 49    Ⓑ 55    Ⓒ 45    Ⓓ 51    Ⓔ 50

**2.** 75  66  57  48  39 ___

   Ⓐ 39    Ⓑ 41    Ⓒ 30    Ⓓ 28    Ⓔ 19

3. **31   46   61   76   91  ——**

(A) 100     (B) 106     (C) 105     (D) 115     (E) 120

4. **20   30   25   35   30  ——**

(A) 25     (B) 35     (C) 40     (D) 45     (E) 50

5. **83   76   69   62   55  ——**

(A) 25     (B) 42     (C) 58     (D) 50     (E) 48

6. **28   39   50   61   72  ——**

(A) 79     (B) 80     (C) 78     (D) 83     (E) 81

7. **6   12   24   48   96  ——**

(A) 100     (B) 156     (C) 129     (D) 190     (E) 192

8. **47   64   81   98   115  ——**

(A) 125     (B) 132     (C) 128     (D) 121     (E) 130

9. **23   33   28   38   33  ——**

(A) 13     (B) 23     (C) 35     (D) 43     (E) 30

**10.** 2   6   18   54   162   ___

(A) 250    (B) 486    (C) 357    (D) 386    (E) 324

**11.** 50   25   30   15   20   ___

(A) 30    (B) 10    (C) 25    (D) 15    (E) 35

**12.** 3   21   147   1029   7203   ___

(A) 30000    (B) 50421    (C) 30317    (D) 53721    (E) 40315

**13.** 63   57   51   45   39   ___

(A) 29    (B) 33    (C) 25    (D) 13    (E) 19

**14.** 19   36   53   70   87   ___

(A) 104    (B) 97    (C) 115    (D) 91    (E) 99

**15.** 14.25   14.75   15.25   15.75   16.25   ___

(A) 16.75    (B) 15.75    (C) 16.15    (D) 15.35    (E) 15.25

**16.** 17   22   32   37   47   ___

(A) 57    (B) 42    (C) 52    (D) 49    (E) 59

**17.** 73   65   57   49   41   ____

(A) 29    (B) 33    (C) 25    (D) 46    (E) 39

**18.** 14   18   15   19   16   ____

(A) 20    (B) 13    (C) 24    (D) 19    (E) 17

**19.** 5   10   20   40   80   ____

(A) 100    (B) 90    (C) 160    (D) 180    (E) 120

**20.** 3   6   12   24   48   ____

(A) 50    (B) 66    (C) 79    (D) 69    (E) 96

# Number Puzzles

In the number puzzles subtest, You are to solve the equations and make both sides equal

**1.** $63 = 9 \times \boxed{?}$

(A) 15    (B) 7    (C) 10    (D) 11    (E) 8

**2.** $23 + 18 = 82 \div \boxed{?}$

(A) 7    (B) 3    (C) 2    (D) 5    (E) 10

32

3. $15 \times \boxed{?} = 60$

    Ⓐ 15    Ⓑ 2    Ⓒ 11    Ⓓ 5    Ⓔ 4

4. $75 = \boxed{?} \times 3$

    Ⓐ 1    Ⓑ 20    Ⓒ 17    Ⓓ 25    Ⓔ 13

5. $84 \div 4 = \boxed{?}$

    Ⓐ 35    Ⓑ 16    Ⓒ 19    Ⓓ 10    Ⓔ 21

6. $32 + 14 + \boxed{?} + 15 = 79$

    Ⓐ 18    Ⓑ 22    Ⓒ 31    Ⓓ 15    Ⓔ 12

7. $5 \times \boxed{?} = 90$

    Ⓐ 10    Ⓑ 15    Ⓒ 18    Ⓓ 9    Ⓔ 23

8. $7 \times 5 < \boxed{?} \times \boxed{?}$

    Ⓐ $4 \times 6$    Ⓑ $5 \times 7$    Ⓒ $8 \times 6$    Ⓓ $9 \times 3$    Ⓔ $4 \times 8$

9. $15 - 15 = 31 - \boxed{?}$

    Ⓐ 15    Ⓑ 47    Ⓒ 31    Ⓓ 0    Ⓔ 62

**10.** $7.5 + 8.5 = 8 + \boxed{?}$

(A) 8.5     (B) 9     (C) 16     (D) 7.5     (E) 8

**11.** $0.45 + 0.75 = \boxed{?}$

(A) 1.10     (B) 0.10     (C) 1.20     (D) 120     (E) 1.25

**12.** $75 - 35 < \boxed{?}$

(A) 40     (B) 32     (C) 58     (D) 39     (E) 20

**13.** $60 \div 3 = \boxed{?} \div 5$

(A) 95     (B) 100     (C) 110     (D) 120     (E) 85

**14.** $56 = 7 \times \boxed{?}$

(A) 6     (B) 8     (C) 9     (D) 10     (E) 12

**15.** $40 \div 5 = 3 + \boxed{?}$

(A) 10     (B) 3     (C) 35     (D) 8     (E) 5

**16.** $3 + 2 + 10 < 18 - \boxed{?}$

(A) 3     (B) 5     (C) 11     (D) 18     (E) 0

**17.** $12 + 7 = 76 \div \boxed{?}$

(A) 2      (B) 5      (C) 4      (D) 0      (E) 11

**18.** $60 = \boxed{?} \times 15$

(A) 4      (B) 2      (C) 7      (D) 6      (E) 1

**19.** $40 = \boxed{?} \div 5$

(A) 120      (B) 350      (C) 210      (D) 200      (E) 150

**20.** $0.5 + 7.3 = 5.3 + \boxed{?}$

(A) 1.1      (B) 2.5      (C) 3.3      (D) 4.2      (E) 1.5

# Figure Classification

Identify the common relationship that binds the figures and choose the right answer

**1.**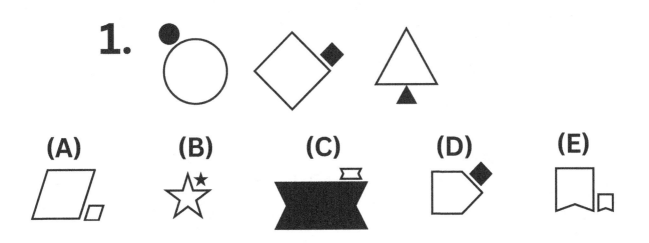

**(A)**  **(B)**  **(C)**  **(D)**  **(E)**

**2.**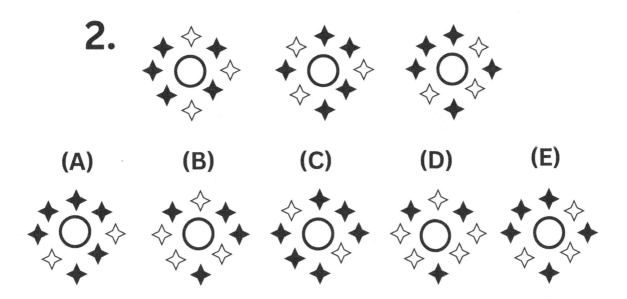

**(A)**  **(B)**  **(C)**  **(D)**  **(E)**

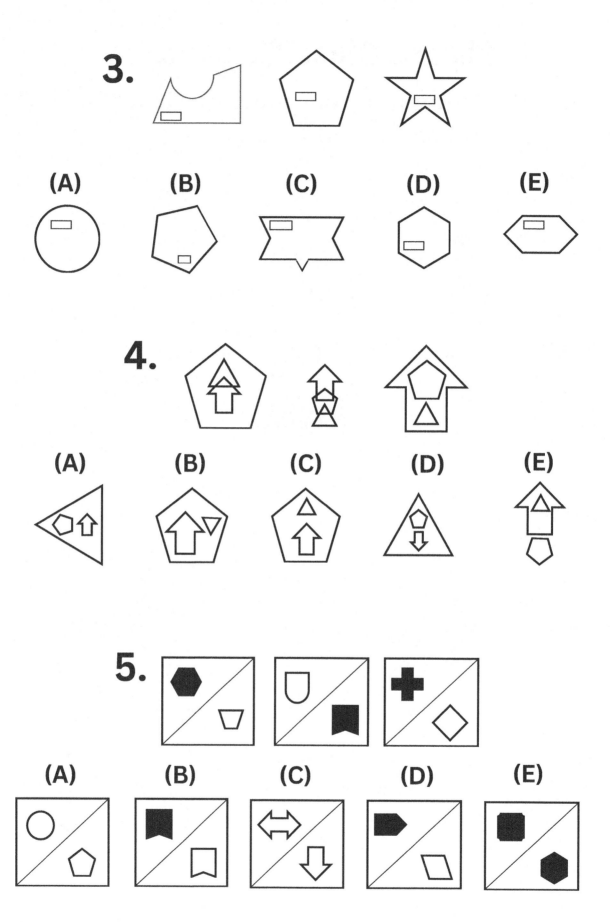

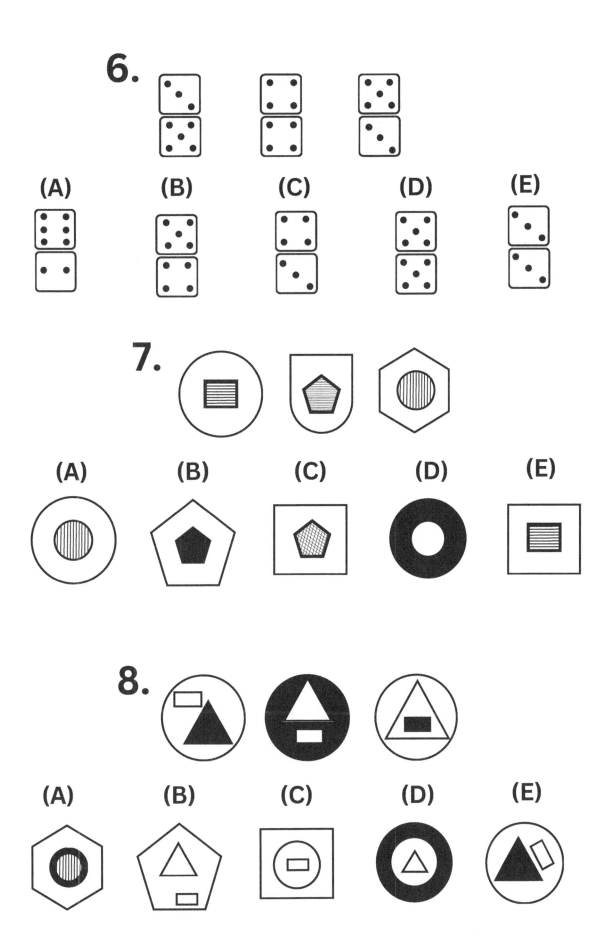

38

**9.**

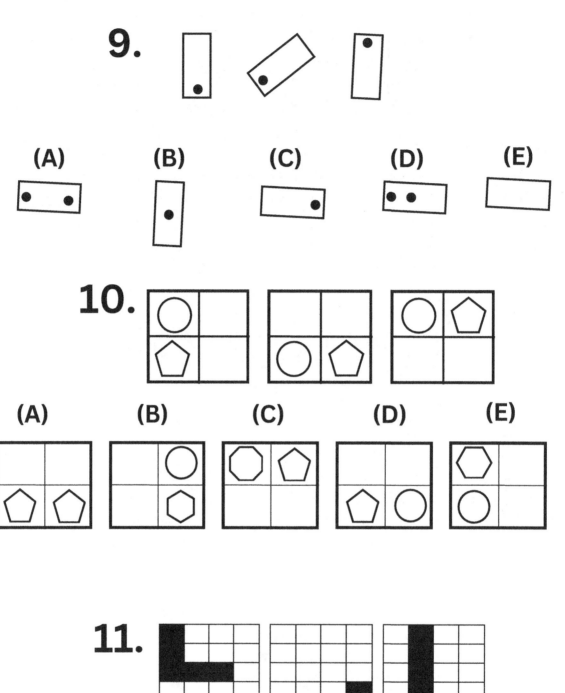

**10.**

**11.**

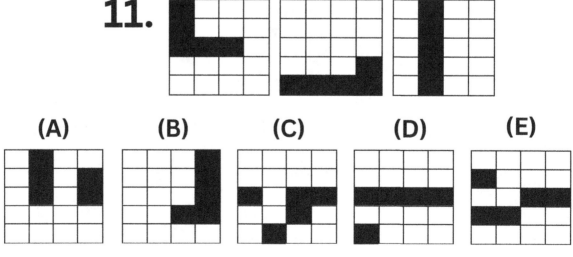

**12.**

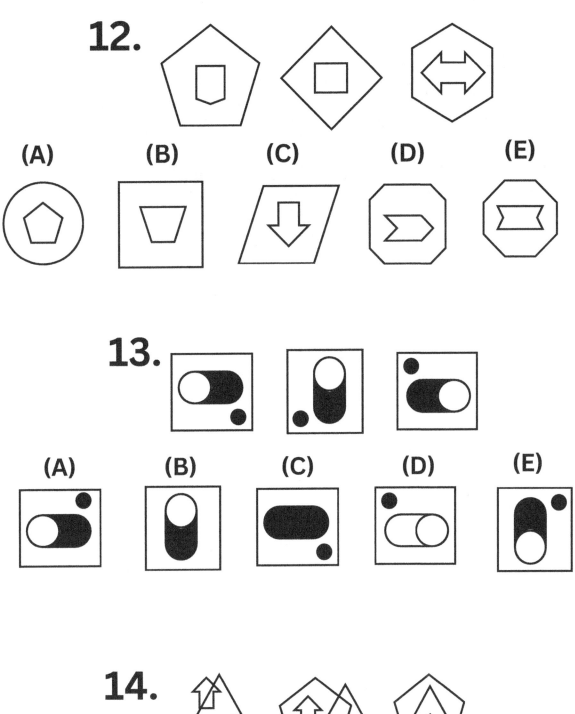

**(A)**     **(B)**     **(C)**     **(D)**     **(E)**

**13.**

**(A)**     **(B)**     **(C)**     **(D)**     **(E)**

**14.**

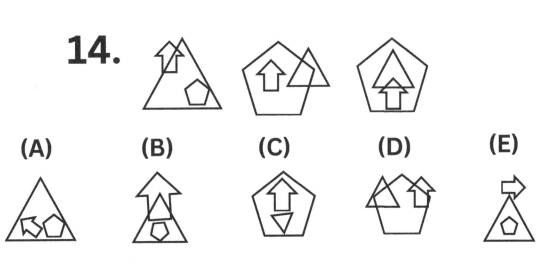

**(A)**     **(B)**     **(C)**     **(D)**     **(E)**

**15.**

(A)   (B)   (C)   (D)   (E)

# Figure Matrices

Find out the connection between the figures in the matrix and choose the right answers.

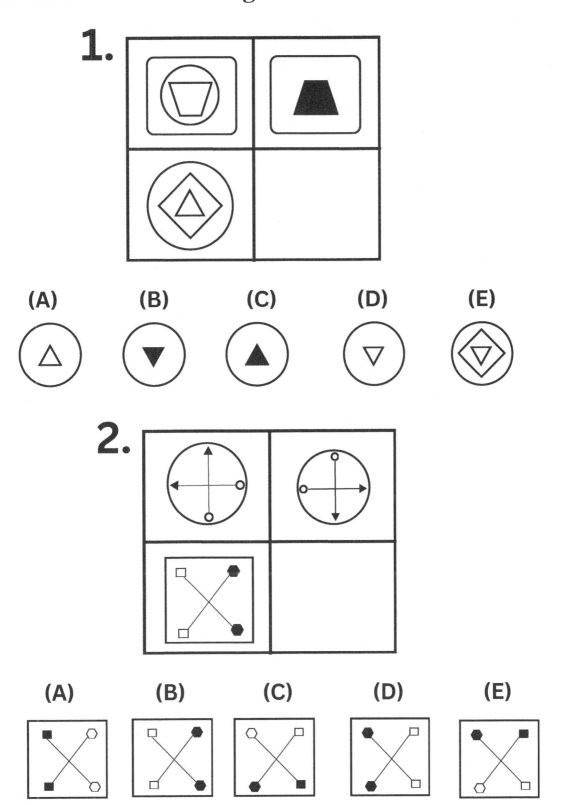

**3.**

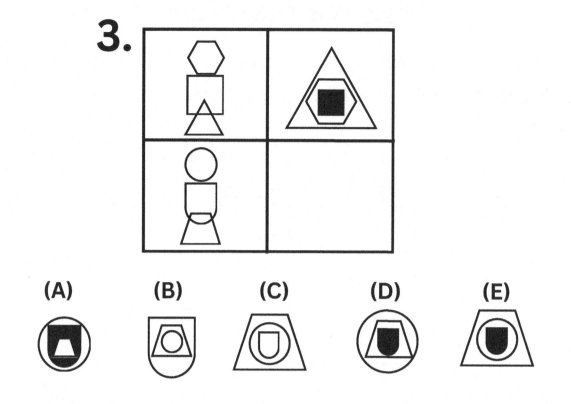

**(A)**    **(B)**    **(C)**    **(D)**    **(E)**

**4.**

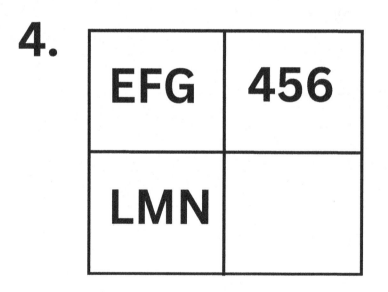

| EFG | 456 |
|-----|-----|
| LMN |     |

**(A)**    **(B)**    **(C)**    **(D)**    **(E)**

**257    135    789    256    578**

**5.**

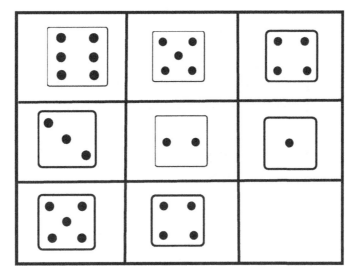

**(A)**       **(B)**       **(C)**       **(D)**       **(E)**

**6.**

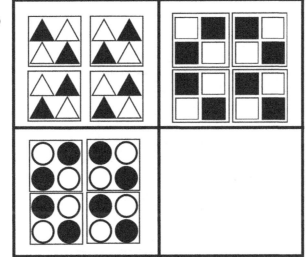

**(A)**       **(B)**       **(C)**       **(D)**       **(E)**

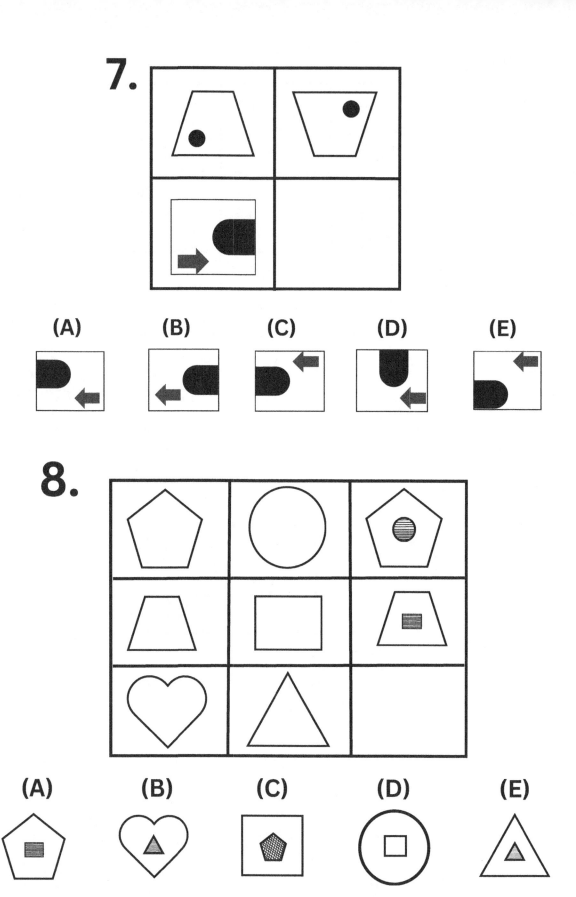

**9.**

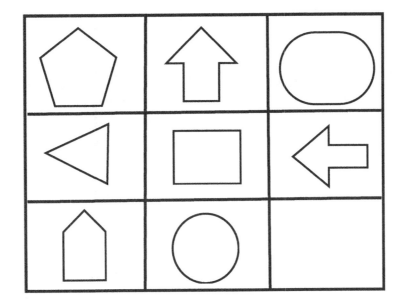

(A)    (B)    (C)    (D) 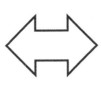   (E)

**10.**

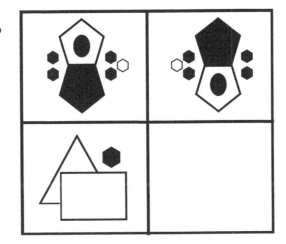

(A)    (B) 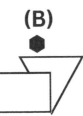   (C)    (D)    (E)

**11.**

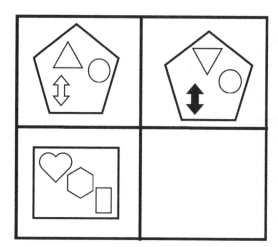

| (A) | (B) | (C) | (D) | (E) |
|-----|-----|-----|-----|-----|

**12.**

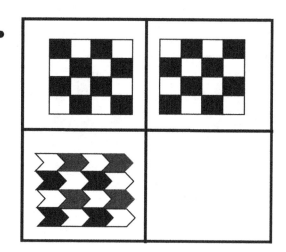

| (A) | (B) | (C) | (D) | (E) |
|-----|-----|-----|-----|-----|

    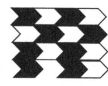

**13.**

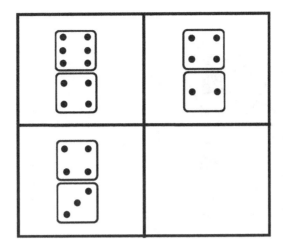

**(A)**   **(B)**   **(C)**   **(D)**   **(E)**

**14.**

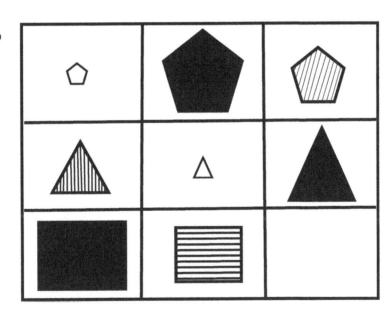

**(A)** 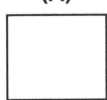  **(B)**   **(C)**   **(D)**   **(E)**

**15.**

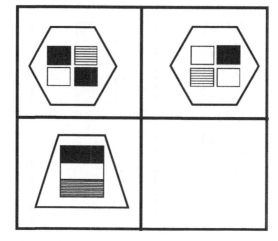

(A)     (B)     (C)     (D)     (E)

# Paper Folding

Figure out how a hole-punched paper will appear when unfolded. Choose the right answer from the options bellow.

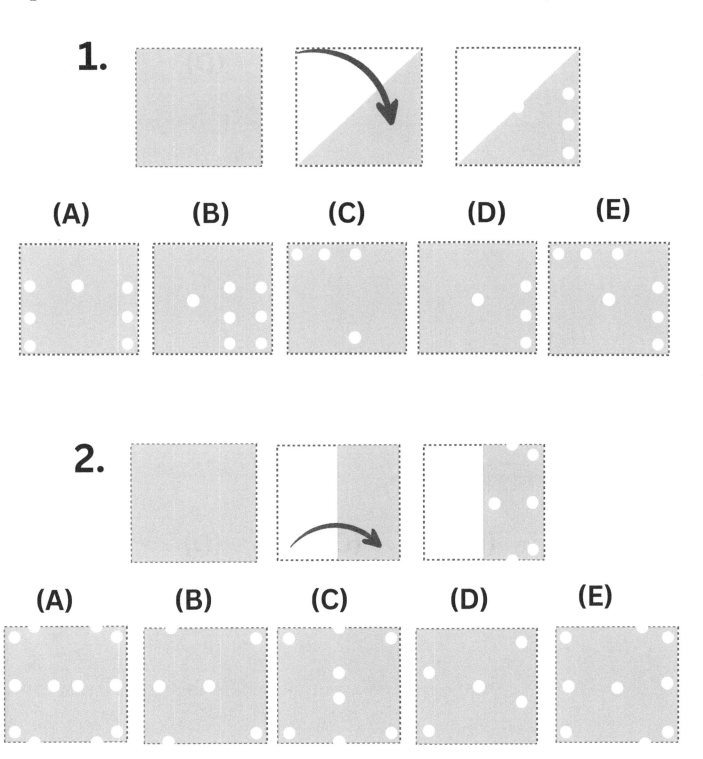

**3.**

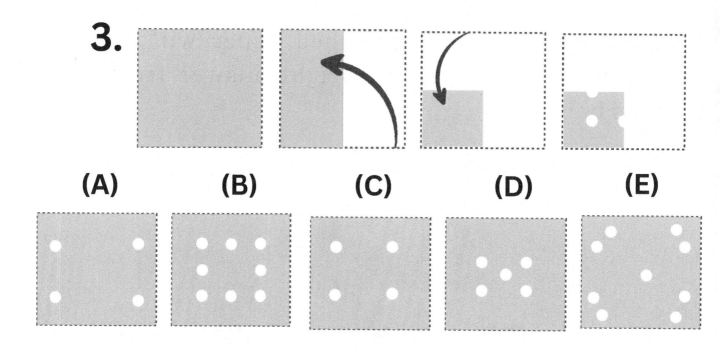

(A)       (B)       (C)       (D)       (E)

**4.**

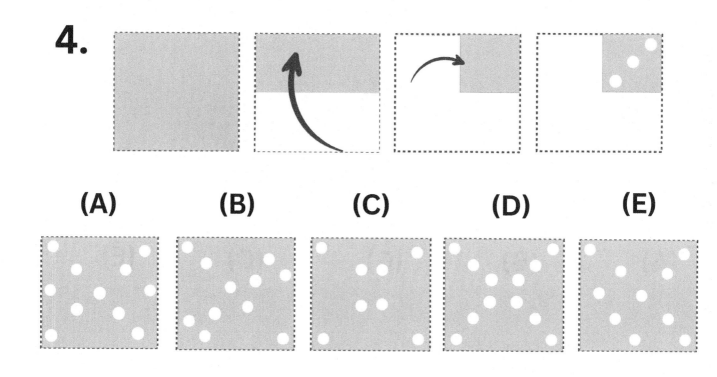

(A)       (B)       (C)       (D)       (E)

**5.**

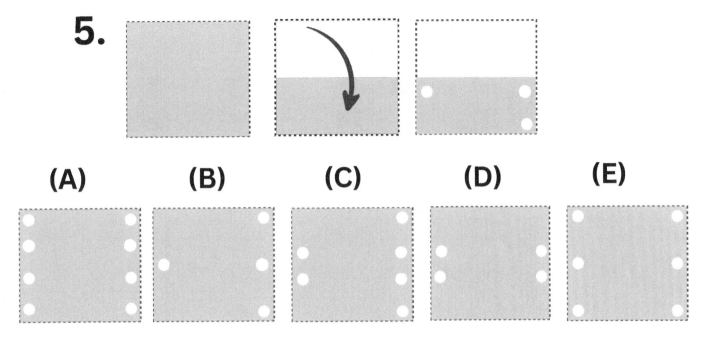

**6.**

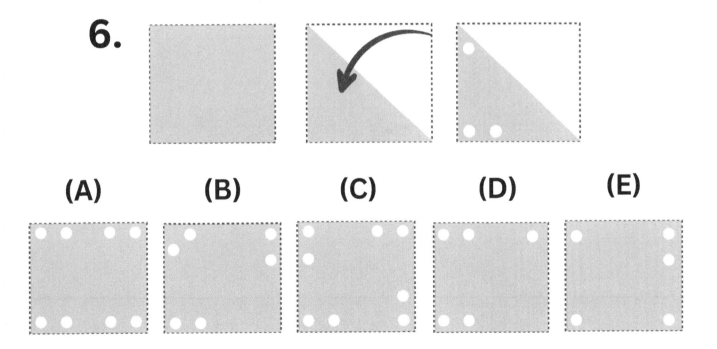

52

**7.**

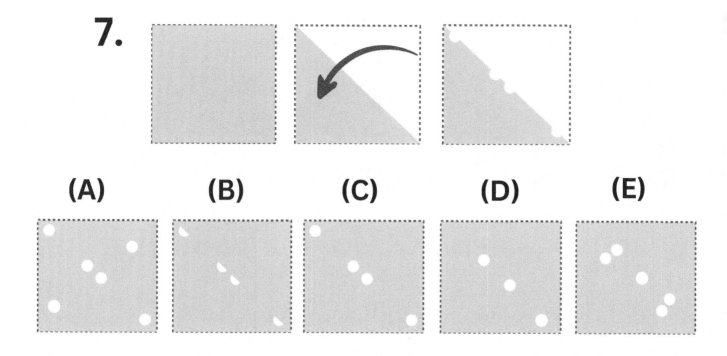

**8.**

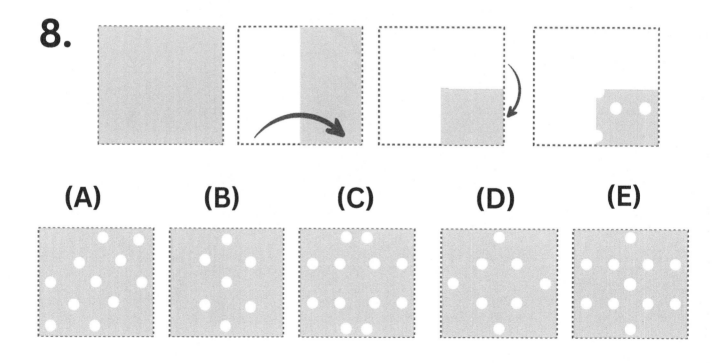

**9.**

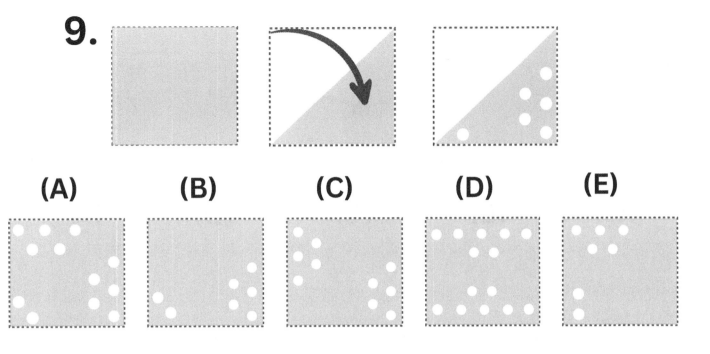

**10.**

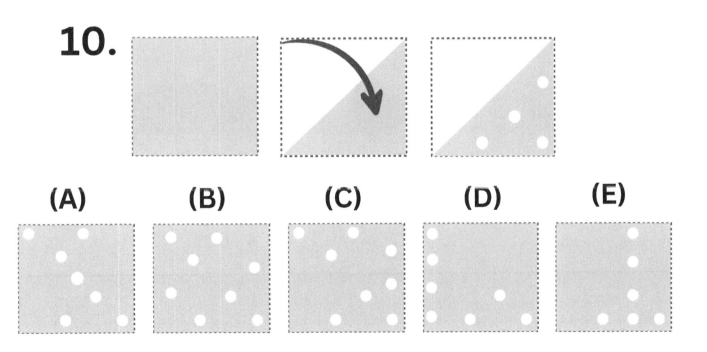

**11.**

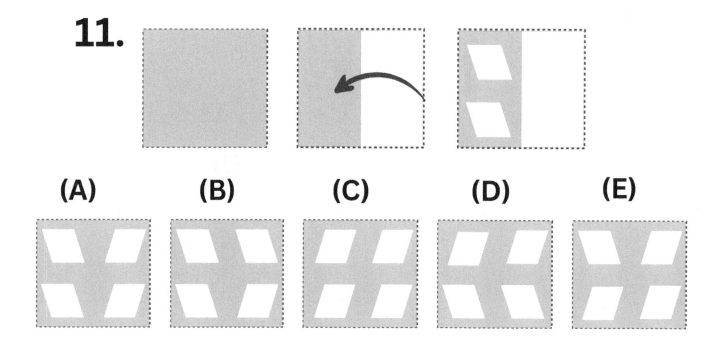

**(A)**      **(B)**      **(C)**      **(D)**      **(E)**

**12.**

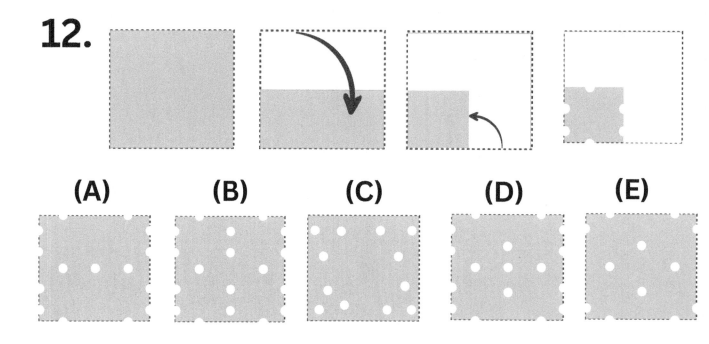

**(A)**      **(B)**      **(C)**      **(D)**      **(E)**

**13.**

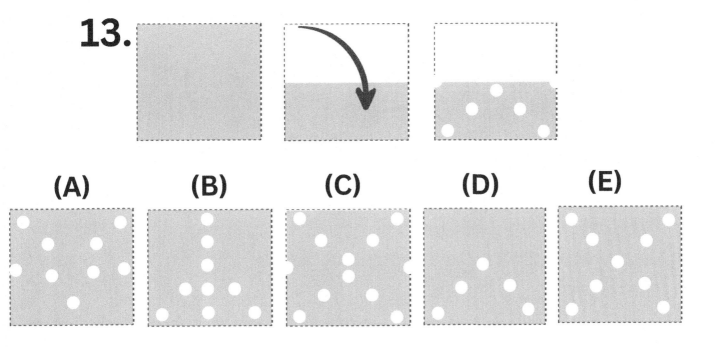

**(A)**  **(B)**  **(C)**  **(D)**  **(E)**

**14.**

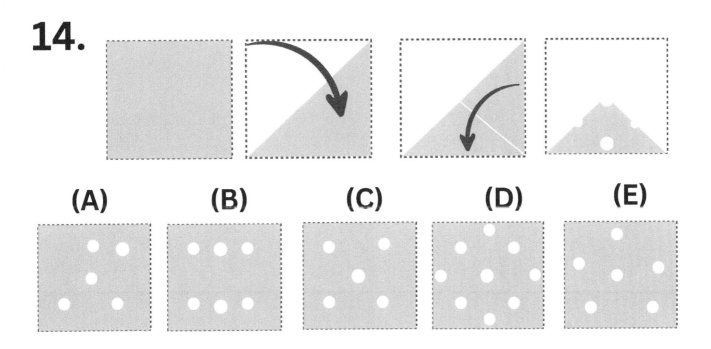

**(A)**  **(B)**  **(C)**  **(D)**  **(E)**

**15.**

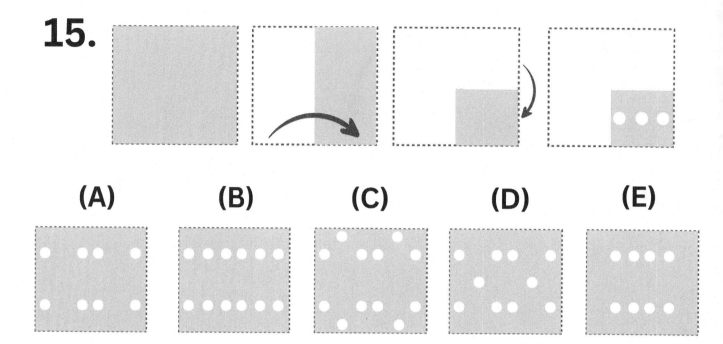

(A)      (B)      (C)      (D)      (E)

# Practice 2

# Verbal Analogies

In the verbal analogies subtest, there is a relationship between the first pair of words. You are to identify this relationship and then choose the pair of words that has a similar relationship.

1. Single ⟶ One : Dual ⟶ _____

   Ⓐ triple   Ⓑ two   Ⓒ three   Ⓓ one   Ⓔ half

2. Trust ⟶ Belief : Rich ⟶ _____

   Ⓐ needy   Ⓑ timid   Ⓒ person   Ⓓ comfort   Ⓔ wealthy

3. Brazil ⟶ South America : Germany ⟶ _____

   Ⓐ England   Ⓑ Canada   Ⓒ Europe   Ⓓ Asia   Ⓔ Africa

4. Ring ⟶ Finger : Bracelet ⟶ _____

   Ⓐ ankle   Ⓑ neck   Ⓒ wrist   Ⓓ head   Ⓔ ear

5. Bicycle ⟶ Cyclist : Pool ⟶ _____

   Ⓐ Fencer   Ⓑ Swimmer   Ⓒ gymnast   Ⓓ skiers   Ⓔ wrestlers

6. Cocoa ⟶ Hot : Lemonade ⟶ _____

Ⓐ warm   Ⓑ boiling   Ⓒ spicy   Ⓓ cold   Ⓔ strong

7. Island ⟶ Land : Lake ⟶ _____

Ⓐ air   Ⓑ sky   Ⓒ water   Ⓓ rail   Ⓔ desert

8. Pig ⟶ Piglet : Sheep ⟶ _____

Ⓐ lamb   Ⓑ cub   Ⓒ calf   Ⓓ kitten   Ⓔ kid

9. Fish ⟶ Gill : Human ⟶ _____

Ⓐ neck   Ⓑ head   Ⓒ intestine   Ⓓ lungs   Ⓔ liver

10. Zebra ⟶ Stripes : Giraffe ⟶ _____

Ⓐ colors   Ⓑ mark   Ⓒ spots   Ⓓ move   Ⓔ run

11. Car ⟶ Garage : Plane ⟶ _____

Ⓐ house   Ⓑ hanger   Ⓒ roof   Ⓓ pilot   Ⓔ airport

12. Poet ⟶ Poetry : Author ⟶ _____

Ⓐ teach   Ⓑ story   Ⓒ create   Ⓓ design   Ⓔ build

13. Pork ⟶ Pig : Beef ⟶ _____

Ⓐ goat     Ⓑ deer     Ⓒ calves     Ⓓ sheep     Ⓔ cattle

14. Cold ⟶ Chilly : Lucky ⟶ _____

Ⓐ joyful   Ⓑ affection   Ⓒ serious   Ⓓ clear   Ⓔ fortunate

15. Hairdresser ⟶ Client : Doctor ⟶ _____

Ⓐ customer    Ⓑ speculators   Ⓒ medicine    Ⓓ patient
Ⓔ team

16. Mouse ⟶ Mammal : Snake ⟶ _____

Ⓐ insect     Ⓑ reptile     Ⓒ bird     Ⓓ cobra     Ⓔ ant

17. Three ⟶ Triangle : Four ⟶ _____

Ⓐ pentagon   Ⓑ hexagon   Ⓒ square   Ⓓ circle   Ⓔ cube

18. Washington DC ⟶ America : London ⟶ _____

Ⓐ France   Ⓑ Canada   Ⓒ England   Ⓓ Spain   Ⓔ Mexico

19. Parallel ⟶ Lines  :  Arc  ⟶  _____

(A) rectangle  (B) square  (C) circle  (D) triangle  (E) cube

20. Speedometer ⟶ Speed  :  Scale ⟶  _____

(A) temperature  (B) height  (C) volume  (D) distance

(E) weight

# Verbal Classification

In the verbal classification subtest, you will be provided with groups of words. You are to identify the word in the given options that belongs to the group of words based on a specific relationship. It could be a category, a characteristic, or any other logical connection between words.

1. Tired, Worn out , Exhausted, _____
    (A) Enormous
    (B) Distruct
    (C) Solace
    (D) Fatigued
    (E) Culpable

2. Brief case, Tote bag, Backpack, _____
    (A) Wallet
    (B) Store
    (C) Purse
    (D) Keeper
    (E) Bundle

62

3. Journalist, Poet, Novelist, _____
   - (A) Nurse
   - (B) Librarian
   - (C) Scribe
   - (D) Accountant
   - (E) Dentist

4. Tiger, Jaguar, Lion, _____
   - (A) Monkey
   - (B) Coyote
   - (C) Dog
   - (D) Cougar
   - (E) Wolf

5. Spanish, French, Italian, _____
   - (A) African
   - (B) European
   - (C) Mexican
   - (D) Asian
   - (E) Englandian

6. Blameless, Guiltless, Clear, _____
   - (A) Culpade
   - (B) Comfort
   - (C) Destruct
   - (D) Difficult
   - (E) Innocent

7. Volcano, Glacier, Earthquake, _____
   - (A) Tsunami
   - (B) Snow
   - (C) Summer
   - (D) Winter
   - (E) Halloween

8. Oxygen, Hydrogen, Nitrogen _____
   - (A) Carbon
   - (B) Carbohydrate
   - (C) Sand
   - (D) Protain
   - (E) Chemical

9. Pleased, Glad, Delighted, _____
   - (A) Irritated
   - (B) annoyed
   - (C) Happy
   - (D) defeat
   - (E) Sleek

10. Inch, Gallon, Ounce, _____
    - (A) Counting
    - (B) Minute
    - (C) Amount
    - (D) Cube
    - (E) Heavy

11. Oath, Verdict, Attorney, _____
    - (A) Debate
    - (B) Talking
    - (C) Witness
    - (D) Receptionist
    - (E) Staff

12. Similar, Comparable, Alike, _____
    - (A) Diverse
    - (B) Distinguishable
    - (C) Varied
    - (D) Analogous
    - (E) Various

13. Garlic, Cassava, Carrot, _____
    Ⓐ Corn
    Ⓑ Potato
    Ⓒ Eggplant
    Ⓓ Cucumber
    Ⓔ Asparagus

14. Reggae, Jazz, Indie, _____
    Ⓐ Music
    Ⓑ Dance
    Ⓒ Country
    Ⓓ Artist
    Ⓔ Musician

15. Persistent, Industrious, Devoted, _____
    Ⓐ Diligent
    Ⓑ Negligent
    Ⓒ Idle
    Ⓓ Lethagic
    Ⓔ Agony

16. Iron, Silver, Gold, _____
    Ⓐ Oxygen
    Ⓑ Strong
    Ⓒ Copper
    Ⓓ Solar
    Ⓔ Jupitar

17. Essential, Crucial, Significant, _____
    Ⓐ Attractive
    Ⓑ Important
    Ⓒ Stunning
    Ⓓ Bright
    Ⓔ Detest

18. Humorous, Hilarious, Comical, _____

  (A) Necessity
  (B) Objective
  (C) Vital
  (D) Laughing
  (E) Funny


19. Kangaroo, Horse, Dog, _____

  (A) Crocodile
  (B) Snake
  (C) Eagle
  (D) Ostrich
  (E) Dolphin


20. Cub, Bunny, Lamb, _____

  (A) Toad
  (B) Calf
  (C) Panda
  (D) Spider
  (E) Deer

# Sentence Completion

In the sentence completion subtest, you are to select the right word to complete each sentence

1. He found _____ for his messy handwriting by Practicing cursive writing.

   (A) beautiful   (B) normal   (C) adjust   (D) remedy   (E) effect

2. Milk and fruits are _____ items that need to be kept in the refrigerator to stay fresh.

   (A) solid   (B) liquid   (C) vegetables   (D) farm   (E) perishable

3. The police officer promised to _____ the case of the missing cat reported by the neighbors.

   (A) analyze   (B) investigate   (C) check   (D) explain   (E) write

4. The dog seemed _____ to come inside the house, Preferring to stay in the garden.

   (A) afraid   (B) reluctant   (C) angry   (D) cheerful   (E) careful

5. In the cooking class, we learned to _____ different ingredients to make delicious soup.

   (A) combine   (B) adjust   (C) remove   (D) filter   (E) duplicate

6. The story had an unexpected _____ leaving the readers surprised and intrigued.

   (A) result   (B) reason   (C) amaze   (D) effect   (E) conclusion

7. The buffet restaurant offers a _____ of dishes, catering to different tastes.
   Ⓐ many   Ⓑ type   Ⓒ variety   Ⓓ different   Ⓐ food

8. The rules of the game were _____ to make it more fair for all the players.
   Ⓐ affected   Ⓑ custody   Ⓒ amended   Ⓓ diverse   Ⓔ engage

9. The _____ of the school increased this year with the enrollment of the new student.
   Ⓐ number   Ⓑ audience   Ⓒ people   Ⓓ population   Ⓔ count

10. Bella felt deep _____ toward her teacher for helping her improve in math.
    Ⓐ Joyful   Ⓑ gratitude   Ⓒ anxious   Ⓓ scary   Ⓔ unique

11. Fruits and vegetables are _____ foods that help keep our bodies healthy and strong.
    Ⓐ pretty   Ⓑ infectious   Ⓒ decent   Ⓓ delicious
    Ⓔ nutritious

12. Solar panels on the rooftops _____ clean energy from the sun's rays
    Ⓐ collect   Ⓑ generate   Ⓒ fund   Ⓓ discover   Ⓔ apply

13. Each type of foods _____ unique; for example. oranges are sweet while lemons are sour.
    Ⓐ tastes   Ⓑ absorb   Ⓒ digeste   Ⓓ delicious   Ⓔ feel

14. Ethan became more _____ in his soccer skills after hours of practice.
    Ⓐ bouyant Ⓑ happy Ⓒ confident Ⓓ dedication Ⓔ ready

15. With a little help, the task became _____ for him
    Ⓐ vitality Ⓑ mysterious Ⓒ furious Ⓓ effortless Ⓔ hard

16. I was _____ at harry's behavior
    Ⓐ fragile Ⓑ enormous Ⓒ strange Ⓓ wrong Ⓔ amazed

17. She felt _____ before the speech, but took deep breaths to calm down.
    Ⓐ cheerful Ⓑ glad Ⓒ bored Ⓓ cautious Ⓔ anxious

18. The kind words from her friend were _____ and made her smile
    Ⓐ tolerate Ⓑ uplifting Ⓒ whisper Ⓓ happy Ⓔ frequent

19. Lucas and Mason _____ this movie last week
    Ⓐ watch Ⓑ wash Ⓒ look Ⓓ watched Ⓔ cinema

20. _____ means loving and respecting your country.
    Ⓐ audacity Ⓑ political Ⓒ patriotism Ⓓ justice
    Ⓔ peaceful

# Number Analogy

In the number analogy subtest, there is a relationship between the pair of numbers. You are to identify the relationship and choose the right answer from the given options to complete the third pair of numbers

1. $[15 \rightarrow 60]$   $[20 \rightarrow 80]$   $[25 \rightarrow ?]$

   (A) 110   (B) 115   (C) 125   (D) 138   (E) 100

2. $[30 \rightarrow 6]$   $[45 \rightarrow 9]$   $[55 \rightarrow ?]$

   (A) 25   (B) 37   (C) 11   (D) 17   (E) 13

3. $[63 \rightarrow 7]$   $[45 \rightarrow 5]$   $[90 \rightarrow ?]$

   (A) 15   (B) 11   (C) 17   (D) 10   (E) 16

4. $[56 \rightarrow 42]$   $[67 \rightarrow 53]$   $[93 \rightarrow ?]$

   (A) 68   (B) 79   (C) 61   (D) 74   (E) 83

5. $[45 \rightarrow 65]$   $[35 \rightarrow 55]$   $[75 \rightarrow ?]$

   (A) 105   (B) 85   (C) 65   (D) 95   (E) 115

6. $[17 \rightarrow 29]$   $[25 \rightarrow 37]$   $[45 \rightarrow ?]$

   (A) 39   (B) 49   (C) 64   (D) 50   (E) 57

7.  $[7 \rightarrow 16]$  $[12 \rightarrow 26]$  $[24 \rightarrow ?]$

(A) 48   (B) 37   (C) 50   (D) 64   (E) 17

8.  $[33 \rightarrow 24]$  $[42 \rightarrow 33]$  $[48 \rightarrow ?]$

(A) 57   (B) 40   (C) 39   (D) 33   (E) 24

9.  $[33 \rightarrow 37]$  $[15 \rightarrow 19]$  $[69 \rightarrow ?]$

(A) 65   (B) 55   (C) 63   (D) 48   (E) 73

10.  $[42 \rightarrow 42]$  $[31 \rightarrow 31]$  $[0 \rightarrow ?]$

(A) 42   (B) 31   (C) 62   (D) 0   (E) 1

11.  $[42 \rightarrow 7]$  $[90 \rightarrow 15]$  $[54 \rightarrow ?]$

(A) 22   (B) 10   (C) 9   (D) 15   (E) 17

12.  $[54 \rightarrow 28]$  $[63 \rightarrow 37]$  $[78 \rightarrow ?]$

(A) 49   (B) 52   (C) 64   (D) 70   (E) 71

13.  $[12 \rightarrow 25]$  $[7 \rightarrow 15]$  $[6 \rightarrow ?]$

(A) 5   (B) 20   (C) 24   (D) 13   (E) 18

**14.** $[5 \rightarrow 35]$     $[8 \rightarrow 56]$     $[12 \rightarrow ?]$

(A) 84    (B) 75    (C) 62    (D) 73    (E) 64

**15.** $[20 \rightarrow 4]$     $[45 \rightarrow 09]$     $[60 \rightarrow ?]$

(A) 25    (B) 12    (C) 18    (D) 40    (E) 35

**16.** $[6 \rightarrow 9]$     $[13 \rightarrow 23]$     $[7 \rightarrow ?]$

(A) 11    (B) 15    (C) 14    (D) 20    (E) 17

**17.** $[45 \rightarrow 28]$     $[34 \rightarrow 17]$     $[58 \rightarrow ?]$

(A) 55    (B) 64    (C) 41    (D) 35    (E) 49

**18.** $[59 \rightarrow 72]$     $[47 \rightarrow 60]$     $[37 \rightarrow ?]$

(A) 50    (B) 45    (C) 62    (D) 73    (E) 30

**19.** $[38 \rightarrow 48]$     $[65 \rightarrow 75]$     $[100 \rightarrow ?]$

(A) 50    (B) 200    (C) 150    (D) 110    (E) 101

**20.** $[15 \rightarrow 45]$     $[7 \rightarrow 21]$     $[9 \rightarrow ?]$

(A) 20    (B) 19    (C) 27    (D) 13    (E) 18

# Number Series

In the number series subtest, you are given a series of numbers that follows a certain pattern or rule. You are to find the missing number in the series

1. 15   23   25   33   35   ____
   Ⓐ 40      Ⓑ 37      Ⓒ 49      Ⓓ 39      Ⓔ 43

2. 124   101   78   55   32   ____
   Ⓐ 22      Ⓑ 43      Ⓒ 10      Ⓓ 9      Ⓔ 17

3. 31   50   69   88   107   ____
   Ⓐ 120      Ⓑ 126      Ⓒ 117      Ⓓ 127      Ⓔ 137

4. 84   71   58   45   32   ____
   Ⓐ 17      Ⓑ 29      Ⓒ 19      Ⓓ 30      Ⓔ 37

5. 15   20   24   27   29   ____
   Ⓐ 30      Ⓑ 32      Ⓒ 35      Ⓓ 38      Ⓔ 31

6. 0   10   7   17   14   ____
   Ⓐ 11      Ⓑ 20      Ⓒ 19      Ⓓ 17      Ⓔ 24

7. 49    43    37    31    25    ____

Ⓐ 17        Ⓑ 20        Ⓒ 19        Ⓓ 29        Ⓔ 18

8. 15    16    18    21    25    ____

Ⓐ 26        Ⓑ 28        Ⓒ 32        Ⓓ 15        Ⓔ 30

9. 0.25    0.75    1.25    1.75    2.25    ____

Ⓐ 2.20        Ⓑ 2.75        Ⓒ 3.25        Ⓓ 2.15        Ⓔ 3.15

10. 14    19    29    44    64    ____

Ⓐ 84        Ⓑ 75        Ⓒ 89        Ⓓ 69        Ⓔ 79

11. 430    380    330    280    230    ____

Ⓐ 200        Ⓑ 150        Ⓒ 130        Ⓓ 180        Ⓔ 210

12. 19    28    37    46    55    ____

Ⓐ 75        Ⓑ 64        Ⓒ 60        Ⓓ 72        Ⓔ 59

13. 33    38    31    36    29    ____

Ⓐ 24        Ⓑ 34        Ⓒ 43        Ⓓ 39        Ⓔ 25

14. 17    17    18    20    23    ____

Ⓐ 25        Ⓑ 32        Ⓒ 29        Ⓓ 27        Ⓔ 30

15. 15   22   19   26   22   ____

(A) 29       (B) 35       (C) 30       (D) 25       (E) 39

16. 48   57   66   75   84   ____

(A) 89       (B) 90       (C) 97       (D) 93       (E) 87

17. 8   22   36   50   64   ____

(A) 78       (B) 69       (C) 75       (D) 68       (E) 80

18. 78   72   66   60   54   ____

(A) 44       (B) 59       (C) 48       (D) 39       (E) 30

19. 28   31   35   40   46   ____

(A) 50       (B) 65       (C) 61       (D) 49       (E) 53

20. 25   32   39   46   53   ____

(A) 57       (B) 55       (C) 64       (D) 60       (E) 49

# Number Puzzles

In the number puzzles subtest, You are to solve the equations and make both sides equal

1.  $12 + 17 + \boxed{?} < 59$

    (A) 20    (B) 35    (C) 42    (D) 31    (E) 47

2.  $50 = \boxed{?} \div 2$

    (A) 150    (B) 110    (C) 100    (D) 95    (E) 78

3.  $\boxed{?} \div 5 = 3 \times 3$

    (A) 12    (B) 33    (C) 45    (D) 22    (E) 15

4.  $18 - \boxed{?} = 18$

    (A) 1    (B) 18    (C) 22    (D) 15    (E) 0

5.  $5000 + 200 + \boxed{?} > 5225$

    (A) 50    (B) 17    (C) 20    (D) 25    (E) 15

6.  $12 + 7 + \boxed{?} = 20 + 7 + 12$

    (A) 25    (B) 19    (C) 20    (D) 17    (E) 11

7.   $48 \div 4 = \boxed{?}$

(A) 16      (B) 8      (C) 20      (D) 18      (E) 12

8.   $48 + 32 > \boxed{?}$

(A) 97      (B) 85      (C) 91      (D) 82      (E) 78

9.   $75 \div 3 = 5 \times \boxed{?}$

(A) 10      (B) 15      (C) 17      (D) 5      (E) 2

10.   $72 = 8 \times \boxed{?}$

(A) 7      (B) 5      (C) 9      (D) 10      (E) 12

11.   $35 - 15 > 10 + \boxed{?}$

(A) 20      (B) 15      (C) 22      (D) 5      (E) 10

12.   $3 \times 18 = 36 + \boxed{?}$

(A) 18      (B) 10      (C) 28      (D) 25      (E) 15

13.   $84 \div 4 = \boxed{?}$

(A) 31      (B) 27      (C) 15      (D) 20      (E) 21

14. $2 + 7 + 15 < 28 -$ ⬚?

    (A) 0      (B) 4      (C) 10      (D) 5      (E) 8

15. $32 - 32 = 13 -$ ⬚?

    (A) 0      (B) 7      (C) 24      (D) 23      (E) 13

16. $2000 + 1000 +$ ⬚? $> 3078$

    (A) 175      (B) 28      (C) 78      (D) 59      (E) 64

17. $15 \times 28 =$ ⬚?

    (A) 320      (B) 457      (C) 242      (D) 420      (E) 330

18. $21 =$ ⬚? $\div 3$

    (A) 52      (B) 63      (C) 49      (D) 74      (E) 37

19. $54 \div 2 = 3 \times$ ⬚?

    (A) 5      (B) 7      (C) 10      (D) 15      (E) 9

20. $12 \times 6 =$ ⬚? $+ 24$

    (A) 48      (B) 33      (C) 24      (D) 55      (E) 12

# Figure Classification

Identify the common relationship that binds the figures and choose the right answer

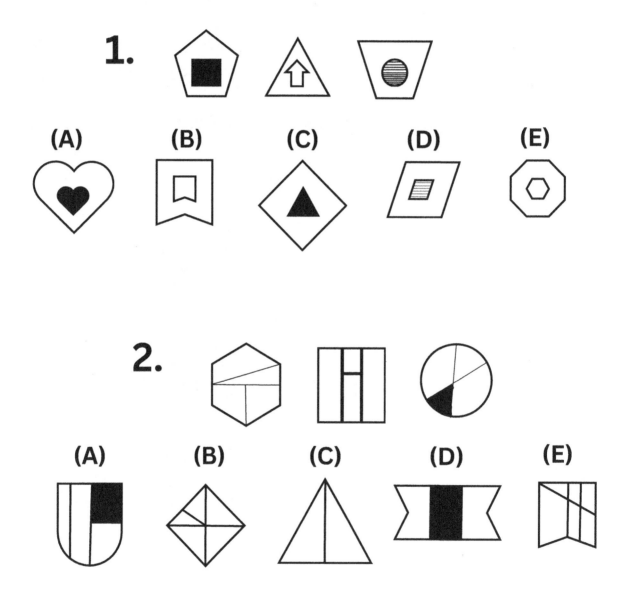

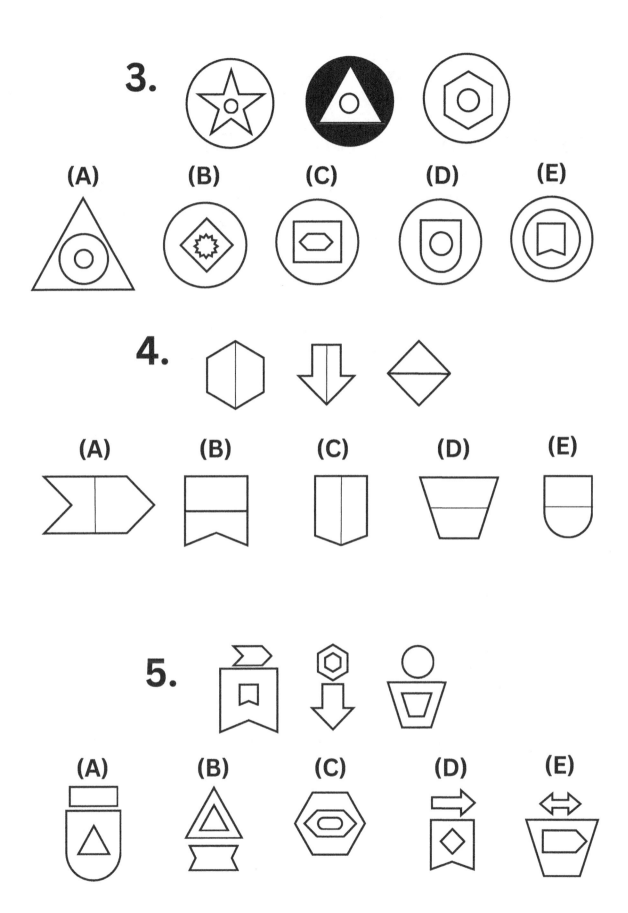

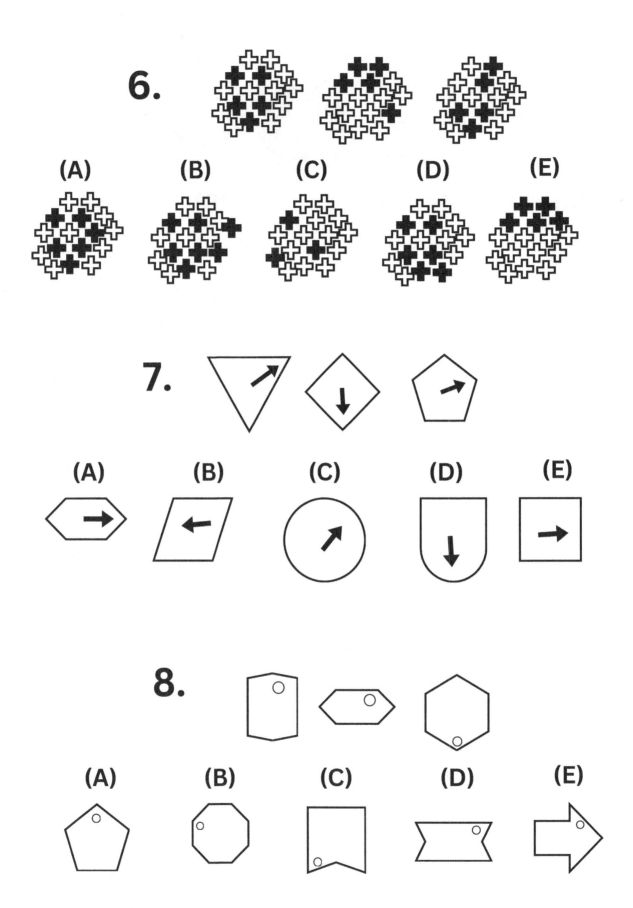

**9.**

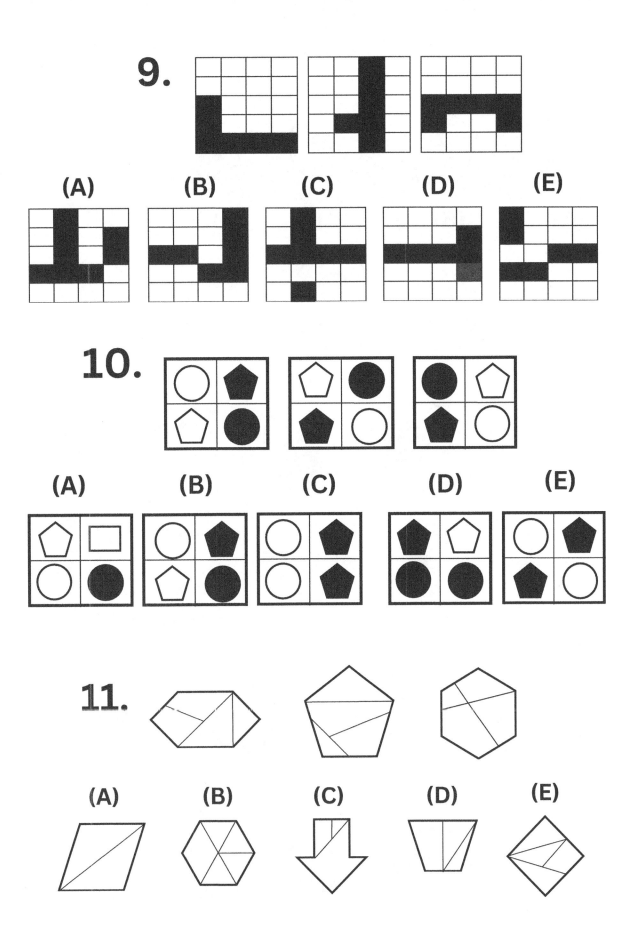

**(A)**    **(B)**    **(C)**    **(D)**    **(E)**

**10.**

**(A)**    **(B)**    **(C)**    **(D)**    **(E)**

**11.**

**(A)**    **(B)**    **(C)**    **(D)**    **(E)**

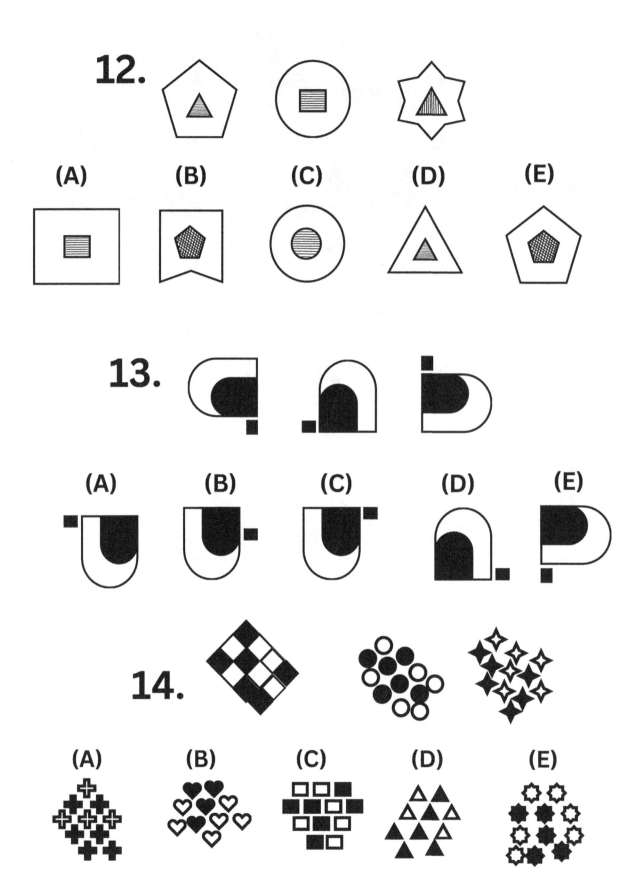

**15.**

(A)     (B)     (C)     (D)     (E)

 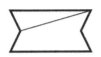

# Figure Matrices

Find out the connection between the figures in the matrix and choose the right answers.

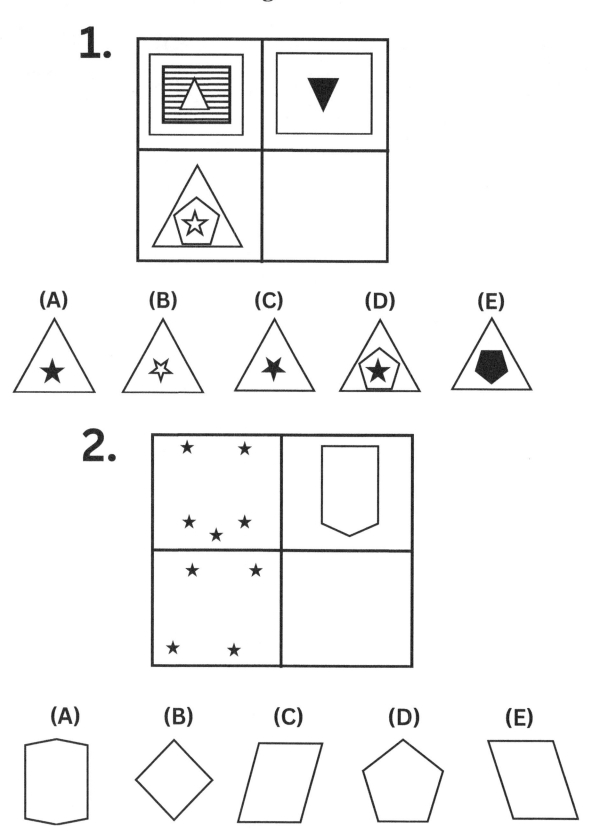

**3.**

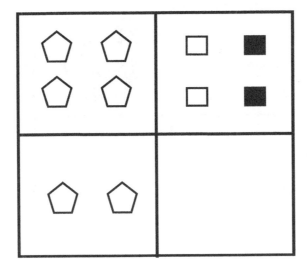

**(A)**     **(B)**     **(C)**     **(D)**     **(E)**

**4.**

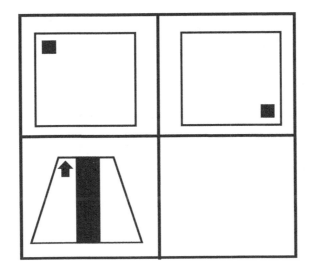

**(A)**     **(B)**     **(C)**     **(D)**     **(E)**

 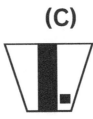

**5.**

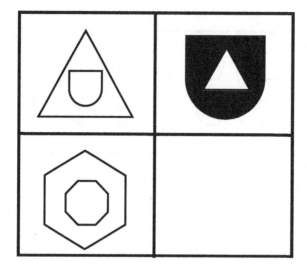

| (A) | (B) | (C) | (D) | (E) |
|-----|-----|-----|-----|-----|
|  | |  | |  |

**6.**

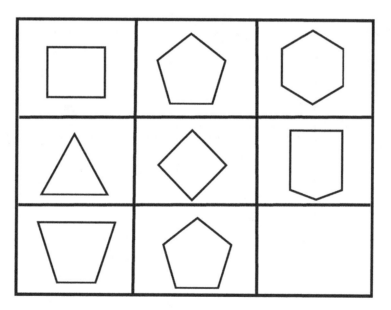

| (A) | (B) | (C) | (D) | (E) |
|-----|-----|-----|-----|-----|
|  |  |  |  |  |

**7.**

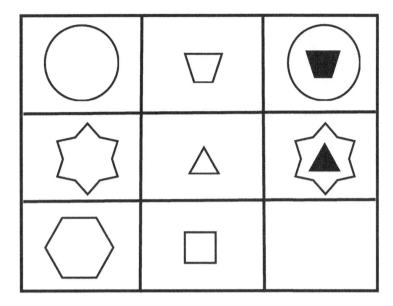

| (A) | (B) | (C) | (D) | (E) |
|-----|-----|-----|-----|-----|
|  |  |  |  |  |

**8.**

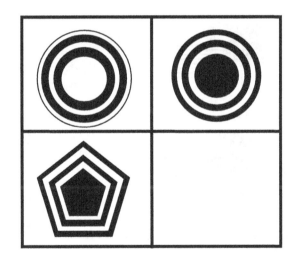

| (A) | (B) | (C) | (D) | (E) |
|-----|-----|-----|-----|-----|
|  |  |  |  |  |

**9.**

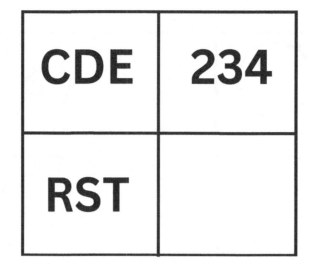

| CDE | 234 |
|-----|-----|
| RST |     |

(A)    (B)    (C)    (D)    (E)

**457**    **356**    **122**    **678**    **135**

**10.**

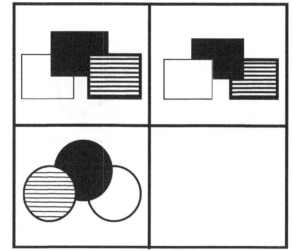

(A)    (B)    (C)    (D)    (E)

        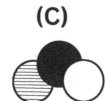

**11.**

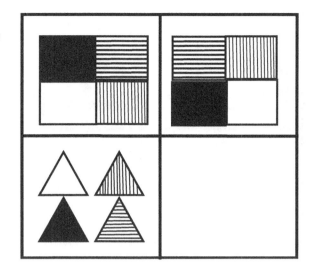

(A)     (B)     (C)     (D)     (E)

**12.**

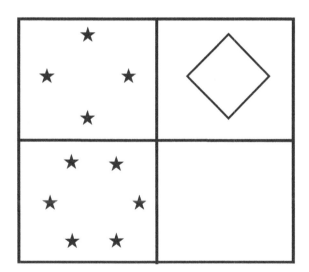

(A)     (B)     (C)     (D)     (E)

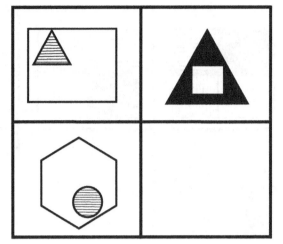

**(A)**     **(B)**     **(C)**     **(D)**     **(E)**

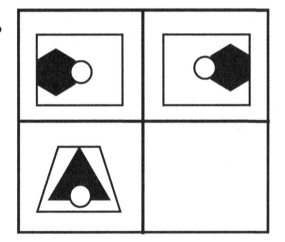

**(A)**     **(B)**     **(C)**     **(D)**     **(E)**

**15.**

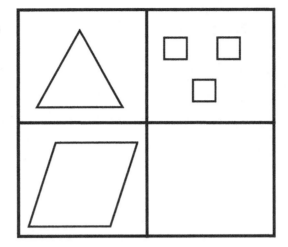

(A)　　(B)　　(C)　　(D)　　(E)

# Paper Folding

Figure out how a hole-punched paper will appear when unfolded. Choose the right answer from the options bellow.

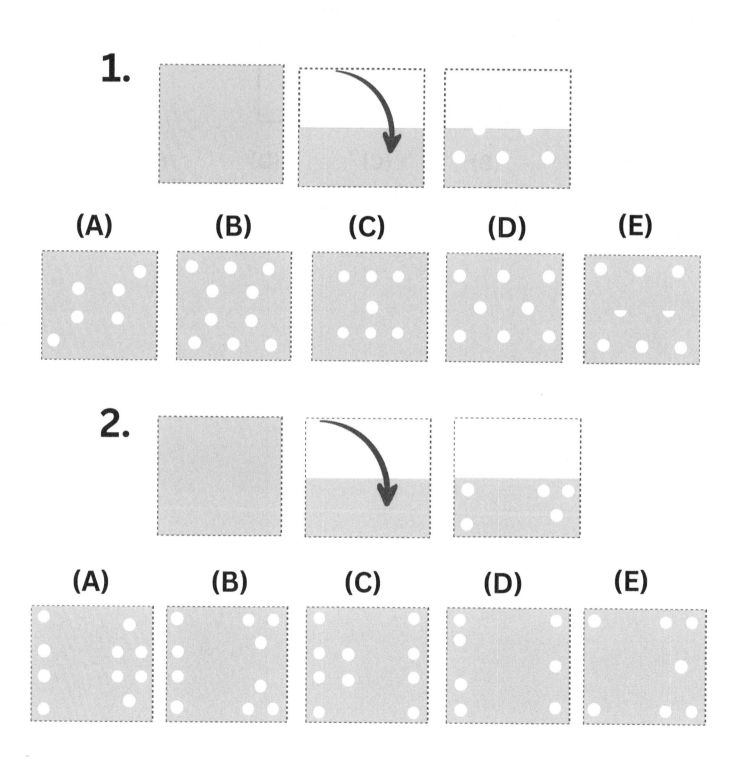

**3.**

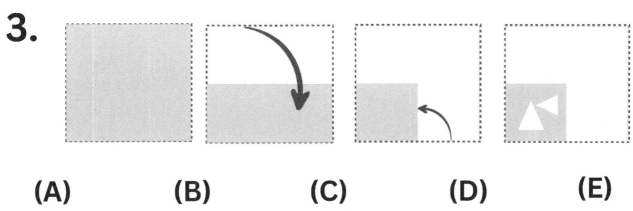

**(A)**      **(B)**      **(C)**      **(D)**      **(E)**

**4.**

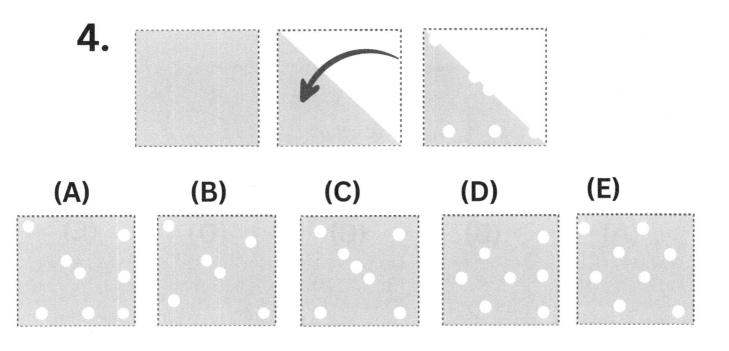

**(A)**      **(B)**      **(C)**      **(D)**      **(E)**

**5.**

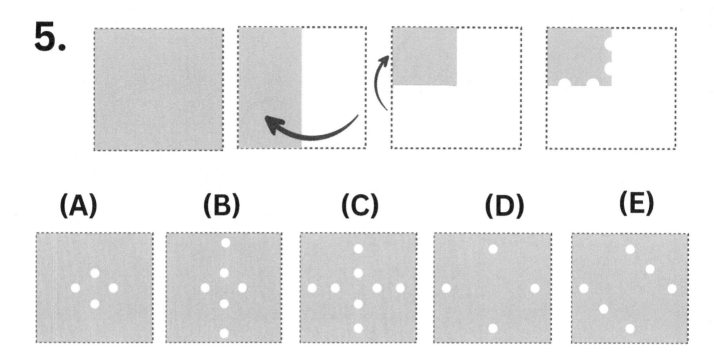

(A)    (B)    (C)    (D)    (E)

**6.**

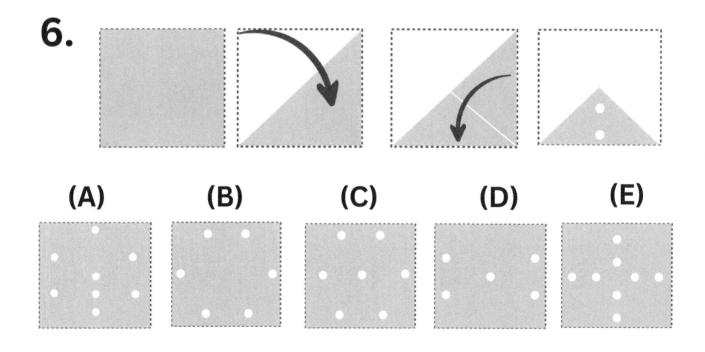

(A)    (B)    (C)    (D)    (E)

**7.**

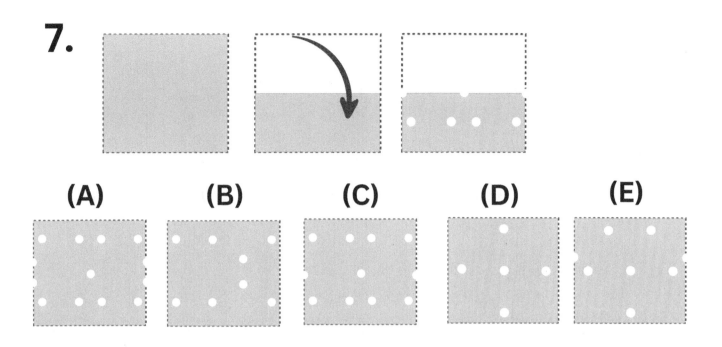

**(A)**    **(B)**    **(C)**    **(D)**    **(E)**

**8.**

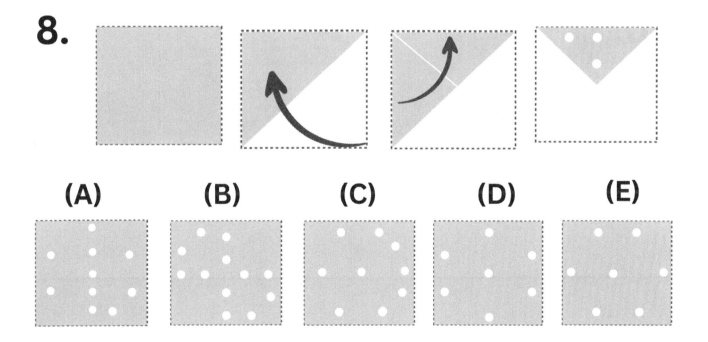

**(A)**    **(B)**    **(C)**    **(D)**    **(E)**

**9.**

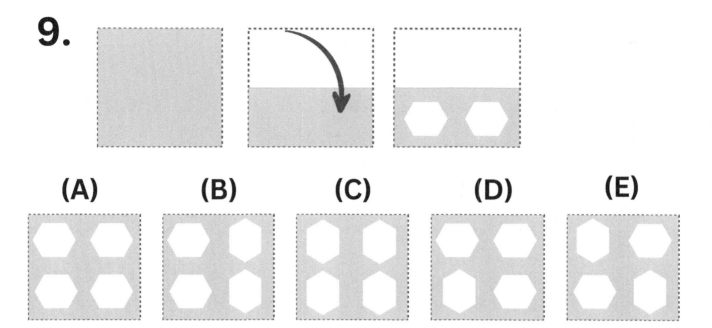

**10.**

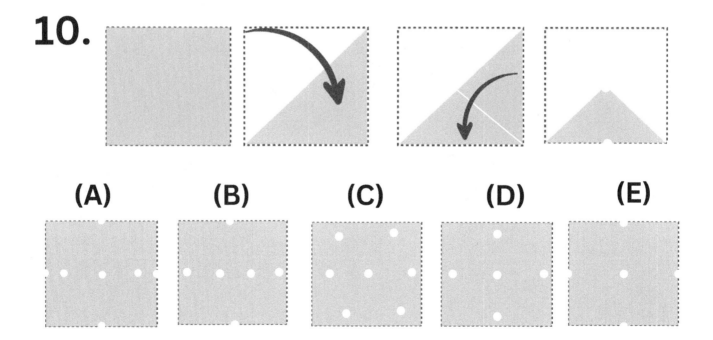

**11.**

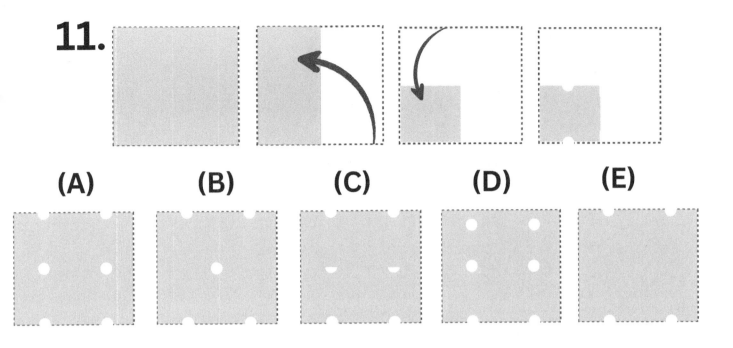

**(A)**　　　**(B)**　　　**(C)**　　　**(D)**　　　**(E)**

**12.**

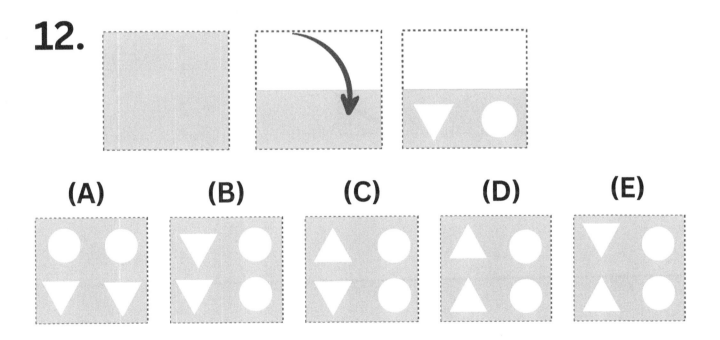

**(A)**　　　**(B)**　　　**(C)**　　　**(D)**　　　**(E)**

**13.**

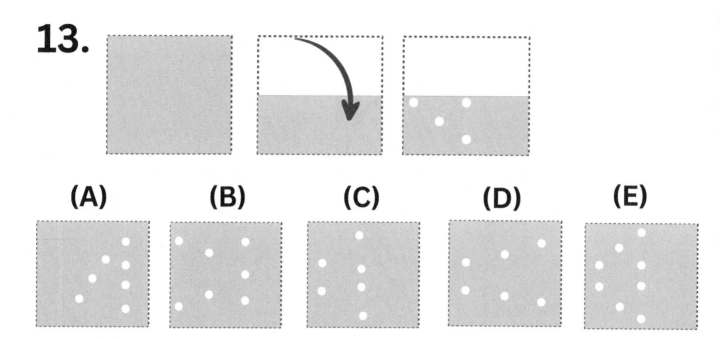

**(A)**　　**(B)**　　**(C)**　　**(D)**　　**(E)**

**14.**

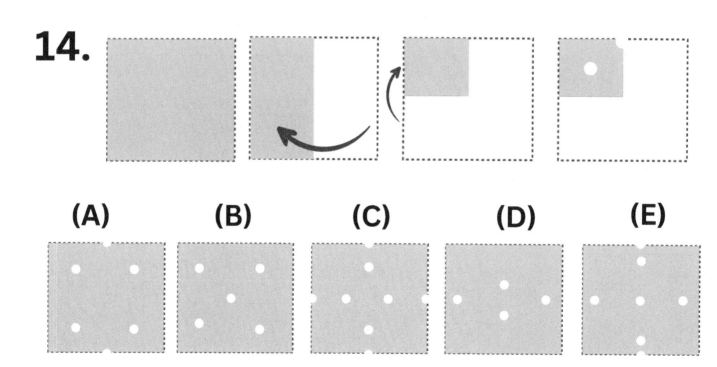

**(A)**　　**(B)**　　**(C)**　　**(D)**　　**(E)**

**15.**

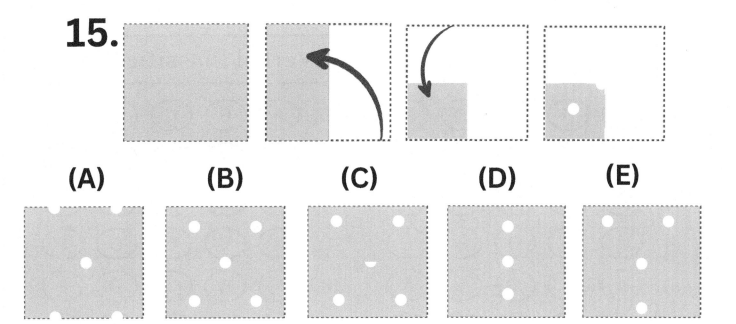

**(A)** **(B)** **(C)** **(D)** **(E)**

# Practice 1

| Verbal Analogies | | | | | | Verbal Classification | | | | |
|---|---|---|---|---|---|---|---|---|---|---|
| 1. | A | B | C | D | E | 1. | A | B | C | D | E |
| 2. | A | B | C | D | E | 2. | A | B | C | D | E |
| 3. | A | B | C | D | E | 3. | A | B | C | D | E |
| 4. | A | B | C | D | E | 4. | A | B | C | D | E |
| 5. | A | B | C | D | E | 5. | A | B | C | D | E |
| 6. | A | B | C | D | E | 6. | A | B | C | D | E |
| 7. | A | B | C | D | E | 7. | A | B | C | D | E |
| 8. | A | B | C | D | E | 8. | A | B | C | D | E |
| 9. | A | B | C | D | E | 9. | A | B | C | D | E |
| 10. | A | B | C | D | E | 10. | A | B | C | D | E |
| 11. | A | B | C | D | E | 11. | A | B | C | D | E |
| 12. | A | B | C | D | E | 12. | A | B | C | D | E |
| 13. | A | B | C | D | E | 13. | A | B | C | D | E |
| 14. | A | B | C | D | E | 14. | A | B | C | D | E |
| 15 | A | B | C | D | E | 15 | A | B | C | D | E |
| 16. | A | B | C | D | E | 16. | A | B | C | D | E |
| 17. | A | B | C | D | E | 17. | A | B | C | D | E |
| 18. | A | B | C | D | E | 18. | A | B | C | D | E |
| 19. | A | B | C | D | E | 19. | A | B | C | D | E |
| 20. | A | B | C | D | E | 20. | A | B | C | D | E |

| Sentence Completion | Number Analogy |
|---|---|
| 1. (A) (B) (C) (D) (E) | 1. (A) (B) (C) (D) (E) |
| 2. (A) (B) (C) (D) (E) | 2. (A) (B) (C) (D) (E) |
| 3. (A) (B) (C) (D) (E) | 3. (A) (B) (C) (D) (E) |
| 4. (A) (B) (C) (D) (E) | 4. (A) (B) (C) (D) (E) |
| 5. (A) (B) (C) (D) (E) | 5. (A) (B) (C) (D) (E) |
| 6. (A) (B) (C) (D) (E) | 6. (A) (B) (C) (D) (E) |
| 7. (A) (B) (C) (D) (E) | 7. (A) (B) (C) (D) (E) |
| 8. (A) (B) (C) (D) (E) | 8. (A) (B) (C) (D) (E) |
| 9. (A) (B) (C) (D) (E) | 9. (A) (B) (C) (D) (E) |
| 10. (A) (B) (C) (D) (E) | 10. (A) (B) (C) (D) (E) |
| 11. (A) (B) (C) (D) (E) | 11. (A) (B) (C) (D) (E) |
| 12. (A) (B) (C) (D) (E) | 12. (A) (B) (C) (D) (E) |
| 13. (A) (B) (C) (D) (E) | 13. (A) (B) (C) (D) (E) |
| 14. (A) (B) (C) (D) (E) | 14. (A) (B) (C) (D) (E) |
| 15 (A) (B) (C) (D) (E) | 15 (A) (B) (C) (D) (E) |
| 16. (A) (B) (C) (D) (E) | 16. (A) (B) (C) (D) (E) |
| 17. (A) (B) (C) (D) (E) | 17. (A) (B) (C) (D) (E) |
| 18. (A) (B) (C) (D) (E) | 18. (A) (B) (C) (D) (E) |
| 19. (A) (B) (C) (D) (E) | 19. (A) (B) (C) (D) (E) |
| 20. (A) (B) (C) (D) (E) | 20. (A) (B) (C) (D) (E) |

| Number Series | | | | | | Number Puzzles | | | | |
|---|---|---|---|---|---|---|---|---|---|---|
| 1. | A | B | C | D | E | 1. | A | B | C | D | E |
| 2. | A | B | C | D | E | 2. | A | B | C | D | E |
| 3. | A | B | C | D | E | 3. | A | B | C | D | E |
| 4. | A | B | C | D | E | 4. | A | B | C | D | E |
| 5. | A | B | C | D | E | 5. | A | B | C | D | E |
| 6. | A | B | C | D | E | 6. | A | B | C | D | E |
| 7. | A | B | C | D | E | 7. | A | B | C | D | E |
| 8. | A | B | C | D | E | 8. | A | B | C | D | E |
| 9. | A | B | C | D | E | 9. | A | B | C | D | E |
| 10. | A | B | C | D | E | 10. | A | B | C | D | E |
| 11. | A | B | C | D | E | 11. | A | B | C | D | E |
| 12. | A | B | C | D | E | 12. | A | B | C | D | E |
| 13. | A | B | C | D | E | 13. | A | B | C | D | E |
| 14. | A | B | C | D | E | 14. | A | B | C | D | E |
| 15 | A | B | C | D | E | 15 | A | B | C | D | E |
| 16. | A | B | C | D | E | 16. | A | B | C | D | E |
| 17. | A | B | C | D | E | 17. | A | B | C | D | E |
| 18. | A | B | C | D | E | 18. | A | B | C | D | E |
| 19. | A | B | C | D | E | 19. | A | B | C | D | E |
| 20. | A | B | C | D | E | 20. | A | B | C | D | E |

| Figure Matrices | | | | | | Figure Classification | | | | |
|---|---|---|---|---|---|---|---|---|---|---|
| 1. | A | B | C | D | E | 1. | A | B | C | D | E |
| 2. | A | B | C | D | E | 2. | A | B | C | D | E |
| 3. | A | B | C | D | E | 3. | A | B | C | D | E |
| 4. | A | B | C | D | E | 4. | A | B | C | D | E |
| 5. | A | B | C | D | E | 5. | A | B | C | D | E |
| 6. | A | B | C | D | E | 6. | A | B | C | D | E |
| 7. | A | B | C | D | E | 7. | A | B | C | D | E |
| 8. | A | B | C | D | E | 8. | A | B | C | D | E |
| 9. | A | B | C | D | E | 9. | A | B | C | D | E |
| 10. | A | B | C | D | E | 10. | A | B | C | D | E |
| 11. | A | B | C | D | E | 11. | A | B | C | D | E |
| 12. | A | B | C | D | E | 12. | A | B | C | D | E |
| 13. | A | B | C | D | E | 13. | A | B | C | D | E |
| 14. | A | B | C | D | E | 14. | A | B | C | D | E |
| 15 | A | B | C | D | E | 15 | A | B | C | D | E |

# Paper Folding

1. (A) (B) (C) (D) (E)
2. (A) (B) (C) (D) (E)
3. (A) (B) (C) (D) (E)
4. (A) (B) (C) (D) (E)
5. (A) (B) (C) (D) (E)
6. (A) (B) (C) (D) (E)
7. (A) (B) (C) (D) (E)
8. (A) (B) (C) (D) (E)
9. (A) (B) (C) (D) (E)
10. (A) (B) (C) (D) (E)
11. (A) (B) (C) (D) (E)
12. (A) (B) (C) (D) (E)
13. (A) (B) (C) (D) (E)
14. (A) (B) (C) (D) (E)
15 (A) (B) (C) (D) (E)

# Practice 2

| Verbal Analogies | Verbal Classification |
|---|---|

| | | |
|---|---|---|
| 1. | Ⓐ Ⓑ Ⓒ Ⓓ Ⓔ | 1. | Ⓐ Ⓑ Ⓒ Ⓓ Ⓔ |
| 2. | Ⓐ Ⓑ Ⓒ Ⓓ Ⓔ | 2. | Ⓐ Ⓑ Ⓒ Ⓓ Ⓔ |
| 3. | Ⓐ Ⓑ Ⓒ Ⓓ Ⓔ | 3. | Ⓐ Ⓑ Ⓒ Ⓓ Ⓔ |
| 4. | Ⓐ Ⓑ Ⓒ Ⓓ Ⓔ | 4. | Ⓐ Ⓑ Ⓒ Ⓓ Ⓔ |
| 5. | Ⓐ Ⓑ Ⓒ Ⓓ Ⓔ | 5. | Ⓐ Ⓑ Ⓒ Ⓓ Ⓔ |
| 6. | Ⓐ Ⓑ Ⓒ Ⓓ Ⓔ | 6. | Ⓐ Ⓑ Ⓒ Ⓓ Ⓔ |
| 7. | Ⓐ Ⓑ Ⓒ Ⓓ Ⓔ | 7. | Ⓐ Ⓑ Ⓒ Ⓓ Ⓔ |
| 8. | Ⓐ Ⓑ Ⓒ Ⓓ Ⓔ | 8. | Ⓐ Ⓑ Ⓒ Ⓓ Ⓔ |
| 9. | Ⓐ Ⓑ Ⓒ Ⓓ Ⓔ | 9. | Ⓐ Ⓑ Ⓒ Ⓓ Ⓔ |
| 10. | Ⓐ Ⓑ Ⓒ Ⓓ Ⓔ | 10. | Ⓐ Ⓑ Ⓒ Ⓓ Ⓔ |
| 11. | Ⓐ Ⓑ Ⓒ Ⓓ Ⓔ | 11. | Ⓐ Ⓑ Ⓒ Ⓓ Ⓔ |
| 12. | Ⓐ Ⓑ Ⓒ Ⓓ Ⓔ | 12. | Ⓐ Ⓑ Ⓒ Ⓓ Ⓔ |
| 13. | Ⓐ Ⓑ Ⓒ Ⓓ Ⓔ | 13. | Ⓐ Ⓑ Ⓒ Ⓓ Ⓔ |
| 14. | Ⓐ Ⓑ Ⓒ Ⓓ Ⓔ | 14. | Ⓐ Ⓑ Ⓒ Ⓓ Ⓔ |
| 15 | Ⓐ Ⓑ Ⓒ Ⓓ Ⓔ | 15 | Ⓐ Ⓑ Ⓒ Ⓓ Ⓔ |
| 16. | Ⓐ Ⓑ Ⓒ Ⓓ Ⓔ | 16. | Ⓐ Ⓑ Ⓒ Ⓓ Ⓔ |
| 17. | Ⓐ Ⓑ Ⓒ Ⓓ Ⓔ | 17. | Ⓐ Ⓑ Ⓒ Ⓓ Ⓔ |
| 18. | Ⓐ Ⓑ Ⓒ Ⓓ Ⓔ | 18. | Ⓐ Ⓑ Ⓒ Ⓓ Ⓔ |
| 19. | Ⓐ Ⓑ Ⓒ Ⓓ Ⓔ | 19. | Ⓐ Ⓑ Ⓒ Ⓓ Ⓔ |
| 20. | Ⓐ Ⓑ Ⓒ Ⓓ Ⓔ | 20. | Ⓐ Ⓑ Ⓒ Ⓓ Ⓔ |

| Sentence Completion | | Number Analogy | |
|---|---|---|---|

**Sentence Completion**

1. Ⓐ Ⓑ Ⓒ Ⓓ Ⓔ
2. Ⓐ Ⓑ Ⓒ Ⓓ Ⓔ
3. Ⓐ Ⓑ Ⓒ Ⓓ Ⓔ
4. Ⓐ Ⓑ Ⓒ Ⓓ Ⓔ
5. Ⓐ Ⓑ Ⓒ Ⓓ Ⓔ
6. Ⓐ Ⓑ Ⓒ Ⓓ Ⓔ
7. Ⓐ Ⓑ Ⓒ Ⓓ Ⓔ
8. Ⓐ Ⓑ Ⓒ Ⓓ Ⓔ
9. Ⓐ Ⓑ Ⓒ Ⓓ Ⓔ
10. Ⓐ Ⓑ Ⓒ Ⓓ Ⓔ
11. Ⓐ Ⓑ Ⓒ Ⓓ Ⓔ
12. Ⓐ Ⓑ Ⓒ Ⓓ Ⓔ
13. Ⓐ Ⓑ Ⓒ Ⓓ Ⓔ
14. Ⓐ Ⓑ Ⓒ Ⓓ Ⓔ
15. Ⓐ Ⓑ Ⓒ Ⓓ Ⓔ
16. Ⓐ Ⓑ Ⓒ Ⓓ Ⓔ
17. Ⓐ Ⓑ Ⓒ Ⓓ Ⓔ
18. Ⓐ Ⓑ Ⓒ Ⓓ Ⓔ
19. Ⓐ Ⓑ Ⓒ Ⓓ Ⓔ
20. Ⓐ Ⓑ Ⓒ Ⓓ Ⓔ

**Number Analogy**

1. Ⓐ Ⓑ Ⓒ Ⓓ Ⓔ
2. Ⓐ Ⓑ Ⓒ Ⓓ Ⓔ
3. Ⓐ Ⓑ Ⓒ Ⓓ Ⓔ
4. Ⓐ Ⓑ Ⓒ Ⓓ Ⓔ
5. Ⓐ Ⓑ Ⓒ Ⓓ Ⓔ
6. Ⓐ Ⓑ Ⓒ Ⓓ Ⓔ
7. Ⓐ Ⓑ Ⓒ Ⓓ Ⓔ
8. Ⓐ Ⓑ Ⓒ Ⓓ Ⓔ
9. Ⓐ Ⓑ Ⓒ Ⓓ Ⓔ
10. Ⓐ Ⓑ Ⓒ Ⓓ Ⓔ
11. Ⓐ Ⓑ Ⓒ Ⓓ Ⓔ
12. Ⓐ Ⓑ Ⓒ Ⓓ Ⓔ
13. Ⓐ Ⓑ Ⓒ Ⓓ Ⓔ
14. Ⓐ Ⓑ Ⓒ Ⓓ Ⓔ
15. Ⓐ Ⓑ Ⓒ Ⓓ Ⓔ
16. Ⓐ Ⓑ Ⓒ Ⓓ Ⓔ
17. Ⓐ Ⓑ Ⓒ Ⓓ Ⓔ
18. Ⓐ Ⓑ Ⓒ Ⓓ Ⓔ
19. Ⓐ Ⓑ Ⓒ Ⓓ Ⓔ
20. Ⓐ Ⓑ Ⓒ Ⓓ Ⓔ

| Number Series | | | | | | Number Puzzles | | | | |
|---|---|---|---|---|---|---|---|---|---|---|
| 1. | Ⓐ | Ⓑ | Ⓒ | Ⓓ | Ⓔ | 1. | Ⓐ | Ⓑ | Ⓒ | Ⓓ | Ⓔ |
| 2. | Ⓐ | Ⓑ | Ⓒ | Ⓓ | Ⓔ | 2. | Ⓐ | Ⓑ | Ⓒ | Ⓓ | Ⓔ |
| 3. | Ⓐ | Ⓑ | Ⓒ | Ⓓ | Ⓔ | 3. | Ⓐ | Ⓑ | Ⓒ | Ⓓ | Ⓔ |
| 4. | Ⓐ | Ⓑ | Ⓒ | Ⓓ | Ⓔ | 4. | Ⓐ | Ⓑ | Ⓒ | Ⓓ | Ⓔ |
| 5. | Ⓐ | Ⓑ | Ⓒ | Ⓓ | Ⓔ | 5. | Ⓐ | Ⓑ | Ⓒ | Ⓓ | Ⓔ |
| 6. | Ⓐ | Ⓑ | Ⓒ | Ⓓ | Ⓔ | 6. | Ⓐ | Ⓑ | Ⓒ | Ⓓ | Ⓔ |
| 7. | Ⓐ | Ⓑ | Ⓒ | Ⓓ | Ⓔ | 7. | Ⓐ | Ⓑ | Ⓒ | Ⓓ | Ⓔ |
| 8. | Ⓐ | Ⓑ | Ⓒ | Ⓓ | Ⓔ | 8. | Ⓐ | Ⓑ | Ⓒ | Ⓓ | Ⓔ |
| 9. | Ⓐ | Ⓑ | Ⓒ | Ⓓ | Ⓔ | 9. | Ⓐ | Ⓑ | Ⓒ | Ⓓ | Ⓔ |
| 10. | Ⓐ | Ⓑ | Ⓒ | Ⓓ | Ⓔ | 10. | Ⓐ | Ⓑ | Ⓒ | Ⓓ | Ⓔ |
| 11. | Ⓐ | Ⓑ | Ⓒ | Ⓓ | Ⓔ | 11. | Ⓐ | Ⓑ | Ⓒ | Ⓓ | Ⓔ |
| 12. | Ⓐ | Ⓑ | Ⓒ | Ⓓ | Ⓔ | 12. | Ⓐ | Ⓑ | Ⓒ | Ⓓ | Ⓔ |
| 13. | Ⓐ | Ⓑ | Ⓒ | Ⓓ | Ⓔ | 13. | Ⓐ | Ⓑ | Ⓒ | Ⓓ | Ⓔ |
| 14. | Ⓐ | Ⓑ | Ⓒ | Ⓓ | Ⓔ | 14. | Ⓐ | Ⓑ | Ⓒ | Ⓓ | Ⓔ |
| 15 | Ⓐ | Ⓑ | Ⓒ | Ⓓ | Ⓔ | 15 | Ⓐ | Ⓑ | Ⓒ | Ⓓ | Ⓔ |
| 16. | Ⓐ | Ⓑ | Ⓒ | Ⓓ | Ⓔ | 16. | Ⓐ | Ⓑ | Ⓒ | Ⓓ | Ⓔ |
| 17. | Ⓐ | Ⓑ | Ⓒ | Ⓓ | Ⓔ | 17. | Ⓐ | Ⓑ | Ⓒ | Ⓓ | Ⓔ |
| 18. | Ⓐ | Ⓑ | Ⓒ | Ⓓ | Ⓔ | 18. | Ⓐ | Ⓑ | Ⓒ | Ⓓ | Ⓔ |
| 19. | Ⓐ | Ⓑ | Ⓒ | Ⓓ | Ⓔ | 19. | Ⓐ | Ⓑ | Ⓒ | Ⓓ | Ⓔ |
| 20. | Ⓐ | Ⓑ | Ⓒ | Ⓓ | Ⓔ | 20. | Ⓐ | Ⓑ | Ⓒ | Ⓓ | Ⓔ |

| | | Figure Matrices | | | | | | | Figure Classification | | | |
|---|---|---|---|---|---|---|---|---|---|---|---|---|---|

| | | | | | | | | | | | | |
|---|---|---|---|---|---|---|---|---|---|---|---|---|
| 1. | A | B | C | D | E | 1. | A | B | C | D | E |
| 2. | A | B | C | D | E | 2. | A | B | C | D | E |
| 3. | A | B | C | D | E | 3. | A | B | C | D | E |
| 4. | A | B | C | D | E | 4. | A | B | C | D | E |
| 5. | A | B | C | D | E | 5. | A | B | C | D | E |
| 6. | A | B | C | D | E | 6. | A | B | C | D | E |
| 7. | A | B | C | D | E | 7. | A | B | C | D | E |
| 8. | A | B | C | D | E | 8. | A | B | C | D | E |
| 9. | A | B | C | D | E | 9. | A | B | C | D | E |
| 10. | A | B | C | D | E | 10. | A | B | C | D | E |
| 11. | A | B | C | D | E | 11. | A | B | C | D | E |
| 12. | A | B | C | D | E | 12. | A | B | C | D | E |
| 13. | A | B | C | D | E | 13. | A | B | C | D | E |
| 14. | A | B | C | D | E | 14. | A | B | C | D | E |
| 15 | A | B | C | D | E | 15 | A | B | C | D | E |

1. (A) (B) (C) (D) (E)

2. (A) (B) (C) (D) (E)

3. (A) (B) (C) (D) (E)

4. (A) (B) (C) (D) (E)

5. (A) (B) (C) (D) (E)

6. (A) (B) (C) (D) (E)

7. (A) (B) (C) (D) (E)

8. (A) (B) (C) (D) (E)

9. (A) (B) (C) (D) (E)

10. (A) (B) (C) (D) (E)

11. (A) (B) (C) (D) (E)

12. (A) (B) (C) (D) (E)

13. (A) (B) (C) (D) (E)

14. (A) (B) (C) (D) (E)

15 (A) (B) (C) (D) (E)

# Answer Key
## Practice 1
### Verbal Analogies

1. A (Lioness is the female of a lion, Mare is the female of a horse.)

2. C (Centimeter is abbreviated as "cm" while gram is abbreviated as "g")

3. E (Just as banana has peel, Nut has shell.)

4. B (Thermometer is used to measure temperature while Barometer is used to measure air pressure.)

5. C (The female of a chicken is called hen while the female of a cat is called queen.)

6. D (Wonderful is a stronger form of good, terrifying is a stronger form of frightening. )

7. C (Cub is the name of baby bear, bunny is the name of baby rabbit. )

8. B (Hexagon has six sides, while octagon has eight sides. )

9. D (Simple is a synonym of easy, complex is a synonym of difficult. )

10. B (France is a type of country while polish is a type of language. )

11. B (Maintain is a synonym of preserve, courageous is a synonym of brave. )

12. C (Teachers teach students, while scientists conduct research.)

13. B (Lizard is classified as a reptile while dolphin is classified as mammal.)

14. E (Brush is a tool used by an artist, scissors is a tool used by a barber.)

15. B (Maternal relates with mother, paternal relates with father.)

16. E (Surprise is a synonym for amaze, affection is a synonym for love.)

17. B (Victory is the opposite of defeat, just as pain is the opposite of relief.)

18. C (Tools. A singer uses microphone to amplify their voice, a tennis player uses a racket to hit the ball during the match.)

19. E (Exhausted is a synonym for tired, cheerful is a synonym for happy.)

20. A (Foe is the opposite of friend while coward is the opposite of brave.)

# Verbal Classification

1.  D  (Type of planet in the solar system.)
2.  E  (All are synonym for triumph.)
3.  C  (Foods that grow underground.)
4.  E  (Reptiles Animal.)
5.  B  (All are synonym for valiant.)
6.  B  (Types of animal with four legs.)
7.  C  (All are types of countries.)
8.  A  (All are synonym for single.)
9.  D  (All are type of grains.)
10.  B  (Positive emotion.)
11.  D  (All are string instruments.)
12.  B  (Months with 31 days.)
13.  B  (All are synonyms for delighted.)
14.  A  (Things you can find in the hospital.)
15.  E  (Mammal animals.)
16.  E  (Same meanings.)
17.  B  (All are type of shapes.)
18.  B  (Different words used to describe teachers or individual who educate others.)
19.  A  (All are synonyms for difficult.)
20.  C  (Parts of an aircraft.)

# Sentence Completion

1. C
2. B
3. D
4. C
5. D
6. E
7. A
8. B
9. C
10. B
11. C
12. B
13. C
14. A
15. E
16. D
17. B
18. E
19. C
20. C

# Number Analogy

1. E ( x2)
2. B ( x4)
3. D (+7)
4. B (+13)
5. A (÷7)
6. B (-23)
7. E (x4)
8. B (÷5)
9. B (+17)
10. D (÷3)
11. E (-50)
12. C (+6)
13. E (-17)
14. C ( x5)
15. E (÷3)
16. A (Second number always 17)
17. B (-11)
18. C ( x2)
19. A (-25)
20. C (+15)

## Number Series

1. D $(+7, +7, +7, +7, +7)$
2. C $(-9, -9, -9, -9, -9)$
3. B $(+15, +15, +15, +15, +15)$
4. C $(+10, -5, +10, -5, +10)$
5. E $(-7, -7, -7, -7, -7)$
6. D $(+11, +11, +11, +11, +11,)$
7. E $(\times 2, \times 2, \times 2, \times 2, \times 2)$
8. B $(+17, +17, +17, +17, +17)$
9. D $(+10, -5, +10, -5, +10)$
10. B $(\times 3, \times 3, \times 3, \times 3, \times 3)$
11. B $(\div 2, +5, \div 2, +5, \div 2)$
12. B $(\times 7, \times 7, \times 7, \times 7, \times 7)$
13. B $(-6, -6, -6, -6, -6)$
14. A $(+17, +17, +17, +17, +17)$
15. A $(+0.5, +0.5, +0.5, +0.5, +0.5)$
16. C $(+5, +10, +5, +10, +5,)$
17. B $(-8, -8, -8, -8, -8)$
18. A $(+4, -3, +4, -3, +4)$
19. C $(+5, +10, +20, +40, +80)$
20. E $(\times 2, \times 2, \times 2, \times 2, \times 2)$

## Number puzzles

1. B
2. C
3. E
4. D
5. E
6. A
7. C
8. C
9. C
10. E
11. C
12. C
13. B
14. B
15. E
16. E
17. C
18. A
19. D
20. B

# Figure Matrices

1. B—The outer shape remains, middle shape disappear, and the inner shape become shaded and rotate 180 degree
2. D—The shapes that are connected by lines inter change position.
3. E—The shape at the top becomes the middle shape, the middle shape becomes the inner shape and became shaded, the lower shape becomes the outer shape
4. C—All figure are in sequential order.
5. D—The figures number decreases by one in the row
6. A—The triangle becomes square, the shaded part becomes blank while the blank becomes shaded.
7. C—The figures rotated 180 degree clockwise.
8. D—The 3rd figure in the row is the combinations of 1st and 2nd row with stripe added to the 2nd row figure.
9. A—Each row has two shapes facing same direction.
10. E—The figure rotated 180 degree clockwise
11. C— The upper shape rotated 180 degree, the lower shape become shaded
12. B—The color inter change
13. D—Two is subtracted from the upper and lower figures
14. B—Each row has 3 shapes, the largest one is shaded, the medium sized one has stripes, and the smallest one is blank.
15. A—The black turned white, stripe turned black and white turned stripe.

# Paper Folding

| | |
|---|---|
| 1. E | 10. B |
| 2. A | 11. A |
| 3. B | 12. B |
| 4. D | 13. C |
| 5. C | 14. D |
| 6. B | 15. B |
| 7. C | |
| 8. E | |
| 9. A | |

# Figure Classification

1. B  The figures has Same big blank shape and small shaded shape.

2. E  The figures has 5 shaded stars and 3 blank stars.

3. B  All the figures have 5 sides and a small rectangle on the inside

4. C  All shapes in the figure are facing one direction.

5. D  All the figures have 2 different shapes on the inside, one shaded and one blank

6. A  The figure at the top is increasing while the one at the bottom is decreasing .

7. C  All the figure have s smaller different shapes with stripes inside a large shape.

8. E  All figures contain a circle, triangle and a rectangle.

9. C  A rectangle with one dot at the end.

10. D  Each figures contain a pentagon and a circle in a square that are divided into 4

11. B  In all the figures, there are 5 shaded squares lined together.

12. B  The outer shape and the inner shape has the same numbers of sides

13. E  All the figures rotated.

14. D  All the figures are facing one direction.

15. B  The total numbers on the dice is 7 in all figures

# Practice 2
## Verbal Analogies

1. B (Single is to one while dual is to two.)

2. E (Belief is a synonym for trust, wealthy is a synonym for rich.)

3. C (Brazil is a type of country in South America continent, Germany is a type of a country in Europe.)

4. C (A ring is worn on a finger, a bracelet is worn around the wrist.)

5. B (A cyclist rides bicycle while a swimmer swim in a pool.)

6. D (Cocoa is typically served hot, and lemonade is usually served cold.)

7. C (Island is a piece of land surrounded by water, while a lake is a body of water surrounded by land.)

8. A (A piglet is a young pig, a lamb is a young sheep.)

9. D (Fish use gills to breathe under water while human use lungs to breathe)

10. C (Zebras has stripes on their body while Giraffes has spots on their body.)

11. B (Cars are parked in garages, while planes are parked in hanger.)

12. B (Poet creates poetry and author writes story.)

13. E (Pork is the meat obtained from pigs, Beef is the meat obtained from cattle .)

14. E (Chilly is a synonym for cold, while lucky is a synonym for fortunate.)

15. D (A hairdressers serves clients by styling their hair, a doctor treats patients to address their health concerns.)

16. B (Mouse is classified as mammal while snake is classified as reptile.)

17. C (A triangle has three sides while square has four sides.)

18. C (Washington, D.C. is the capital city of the United states while London is the capital city of England .)

19. C (Parallel is related to lines, Arc is related to circles.)

20. E (Speedometer helps to measure speed while a scale helps measure the weight of an object.)

# Verbal Classification

1. D  (All words meaning are the same.)
2. C  (All are types of bags.)
3. C  (These jobs are all about writing.)
4. D  (All animals belongs to cat family.)
5. C  (They are related to country.)
6. E  (All are synonym for innocent.)
7. A  (All are natural disasters.)
8. A  (All are types of elements.)
9. C  (All are synonyms for pleased.)
10. B  (All are units of measurements.)
11. C  (All are terms use in court of law.)
12. D  (All words meaning are the same.)
13. B  (All are root vegetables.)
14. C  (Music genres.)
15. A  (These words are used to talk about someone who works hard and is committed to doing a good job)
16. C  (All are types of metals.)
17. B  (Synonym for essential .)
18. E  (All are synonym for funny.)
19. E  (All are mammal animals.)
20. B  (All are young animals.)

# Sentence Completion

1. D
2. E
3. B
4. B
5. A
6. E
7. C
8. C
9. D
10. B
11. E
12. B
13. A
14. C
15. D
16. E
17. E
18. B
19. D
20. C

# Number Analogy

1. E (×4)
2. C (÷5)
3. D (÷9)
4. B (-14)
5. D (+20)
6. E (+12)
7. C (×2,+2)
8. C (-9)
9. E (+4)
10. D (First and second numbers are the same)
11. C (÷6)
12. B (-26)
13. D (×2, +1)
14. A (× 7)
15. B (÷ 5)
16. A (×2, -3)
17. C (-17)
18. A (+13)
19. D (+10)
20. C (×3)

# Number Series

1. E (+8,+2,+8,+2,+8)
2. D (-23,-23,-23,-23,-23)
3. B (+19,+19,+19,+19,+19)
4. C (-13,-13,-13,-13,-13)
5. A (+5,+4,+3,+2,+1)
6. E (+10,-3,+10,-3,+10)
7. C (-6,-6,-6,-6,-6)
8. E (+1,+2,+3,+4,+5)
9. B (+0.5,+0.5,+0.5,+0.5,+0.5)
10. C (+5,+10,+15,+20,+25)
11. D (-50,-50,-50,-50,-50)
12. B (+9,+9,+9,+9,+9)
13. B (+5,-7,+5,-7,+5)
14. D (+0,+1,+2,+3,+4)
15. C (+7,-3,+7,-3,+7)
16. D (+9,+9,+9,+9,+9)
17. A (+14,+14,+14,+14,+14)
18. C (-6,-6,-6,-6,-6)
19. E (+3,+4,+5,+6,+7)
20. D (+7,+7,+7,+7,+7)

# Number puzzles

1. A
2. C
3. C
4. E
5. A
6. C
7. E
8. E
9. D
10. C
11. D
12. A
13. E
14. A
15. E
16. A
17. D
18. B
19. E
20. A

# Figure Matrices

1. C – The middle shape disappear, the outer shape remains, the inner shape becomes shaded and rotate 180 degree.
2. C – Stars are placed at the joint of the figures
3. B – The pentagon change to square and the right side square becomes shaded
4. E – The figure rotated 180 degree clockwise.
5. D – The outer shape becomes the inner shape and the inner shapes become the outer shape and shaded.
6. C – The side of the shapes increases by one across the rows.
7. E – Third row is the combination of the shapes in first and second rows, and the shapes in the 2nd row becomes shaded.
8. A – The colors in the figure inter change.
9. D – All the figures are in sequential order.
10. C – The striped square moved from front to the back, while the blank square moved from the back to the front.
11. B – The figures move anti clockwise.
12. D – The stars are placed at the joint of the figures.
13. B – The outer square shape becomes the inner shape while the striped triangle becomes shaded and the outer shape.
14. A – The figures rotated 180 degree.
15. C – The numbers of the sides of the shape is the number of the square in the second row.

# Paper Folding

1. D
2. A
3. B
4. A
5. C
6. E
7. C
8. B
9. A
10. E
11. A
12. C
13. E
14. A
15. B

# Figure Classification

1. C   All the figures has different outer and inner shapes.

2. A   All the figures are divided into 4 parts.

3. D   All the figures have 3 shapes, a circle on the inside, different shapes in the middle and another circle on the outside.

4. C   All figures are divided into two equal parts.

5. B   All the figures has two same shapes and one different shapes.

6. E   All the figures has five shaded plus shapes.

7. A   In all the figures, there is an arrow pointing towards the corner sides of the shapes.

8. D   All the figures has 6 sides and circle inside.

9. D   All the figures have 6 shaded squares lined together.

10. B   The figures has two pentagons, one shaded and one blank. Two circles, one shaded and one blank

11. E   All the figures are divided into 4 parts.

12. B   The outer shape and inner shape are different.

13. C   All the figures rotated.

14. C   All the figures have same numbers of blank and shade shapes.

15. D   All the figures are divided into two equal parts by a diagonal line.

Made in United States
North Haven, CT
22 March 2025

67106417R00070